Maurice Durant, Volume I

Charles Garvice

BIBLIOLIFE

Maurice Durant.

BY

CHARLES GARVICE,

AUTHOR OF "ONLY COUNTRY LOVE," "EVE," &C.

VOL. I.

LONDON:

A. SMITH, 334, STRAND, W.C.

1875.

TO

HENRY IRVING,

WITH THE

WARMEST ADMIRATION

AND ESTEEM.

PREFACE.

PREFACES are out of date, but I may
be permitted, here, to state that this Novel
of Incident was written some years ago when
the Author's acquaintance with the world,
the flesh, and His Satanic Majesty was small
in degree and imaginative in quality. The
story was first published in a periodical, and,
notwithstanding its too palpable inconsis-
tencies and crudity, obtained a fair share of
success. That success is the cause of its
republication in this form. While reading
the proofs for this edition I attempted to

prune and revise; but the attempt proved, at the outset, that the wiser course would be to resign the imperfect whole to the critics, who, in their tenderness for all things young —not to say vernal—may, perchance, temper justice with mercy.

CHARLES GARVICE.

The Retreat, Cookham,
Aug. 24th, 1875.

CHAPTER I.

Dreams, books, are each a world; and books, we know,
 Are a substantial world, both pure and good;
Round these, with tendrils strong as flesh and blood,
 Our pastime and our happiness will grow.
WORDSWORTH.

WHAT need is there to describe Grassmere? Who does not know it, with its half dozen rustic houses, handful of farms, irregular cluster of cottages, old, time-eaten church, rotting pillory and rusty stocks; its bright, silver stream, tall, regal trees, green-robed valleys, and heather-covered hills; and, lastly, its ancient, stately Hall and moss-grown Rectory?

Our English rural villages are very much alike, and between Grassmere and any other of the thousand and one English hamlets there is but little or no difference. Perhaps it

B

might boast—for every village, no matter how small, boasts of something—of its old Hall and of the ancient blood of the people who held it, and in doing so it would not be vaunting without cause, for Chichester Hall was a noble pile, honoured by age and a perfect halo of historic memories.

Artists travelled far and from all corners of the civilised world to gaze ecstatically upon its antique beauties, and transfer its left wing, right wing, and its noble *façade* to their bulky sketch books. The greatest poet of the day had visited it and made it the scene of one of his greatest songs; and antiquarians, when discussing its age, beauties, and history, were wont to grow eloquent and declare that it was the purest specimen of old English mansions.

With all this to back them the Grassmerians may be excused in looking upon their Hall as the greatest piece of glory in brick and stone under the sun.

The present owner of the Hall, Sir Fielding

Chichester, was as proud of the majestic pile as the villagers who dwelt outside its gates. He loved every inch of it, from musty cellar to carven chimney-stack, and could have told, had he chosen to do so, its whole history, from the day when Luke Chichester laid the huge foundation stone with his own hands—which were scarcely cleansed of the blood spent in the late wars of King Charles the Unfortunate —to the present time, when its grim walls and corridors were lightened by crimson damask and statuary, and the sunlight of peaceful happiness shone through its stained windows.

But Sir Fielding Chichester would not have chosen to have told it, for he spoke but little, and then only of his books, for Sir Fielding lived and had his being only in the spacious library of the Hall. There you could find him almost the whole day through, and very often all night. There, between four high book-lined walls, the owner of a vast and beautiful estate, the possessor of an ancient name and an enormous county influence, the father of a hand-some, noble-hearted son and lovely daughter, spent his life. It was his world; in no other air save that filled with the odour of Russia leather and time-stained parchment could he breathe happily. In nothing but the absolute silence of the vast library, with its double doors and thickly painted windows, could he be at ease, and in no friend—not even in his beloved children—could he find that comfort and companionship which the silent record of the mighty dead opened up to him.

Yet let not our readers misunderstand the man. He was no mere bookworm, blindly creeping through the mountain of knowledge; no shrunken student in snuff-stained and neglected attire. No, these almost inevitable consequences of such a life in another man were averted in Sir Fielding Chichester by the old blue blood which kept him, no matter what, in habits a perfect gentleman, even to the tying of his cravat.

Slightly bent, yet still looking tall, with pale face and clear-cut features, keen, bright eyes and lofty forehead, small handed and footed, he could have held his head up in point of aristocratic appearance even with the Charles Chichester whose kingly form shone down from its gilt frame in the picture gallery outside his library door.

With such ancestors it was little wonder that Chudleigh Chichester should be both *distingué* looking and handsome. He was of rather larger build than Sir Fielding, with fair hair and dark eyes. That there was a look of firmness about the lower part of his face, and an air of thoughtful determination upon the white forehead were matters of congratulation, considering that the whole care of the estates fell upon his broad shoulders.

Everything was left to Chudleigh, and had been since he was of an age to understand the steward's books, and the nature of a landlord's duties.

He was now twenty-three years old, though looking younger, being fair, good-looking, as we have said, and heart free, save for the affection he bore his father, and the great love he poured out on his sister Maud, the belle of the county, and the object of Grassmere's adoration.

We have experienced comparatively little difficulty in describing one small portion of the Chichester family, but as our pen writes " Maud " it falters and stops motionless and powerless to describe the vision of beautiful purity which memory calls up. If we may say that her face was a perfect oval, her eyes dark, deep, and as clear and fine as the dew upon a rose, her mouth perfect and bud-like, and her hair a marvellous shower of silken light, how nearer are we to producing sweet Maud Chichester than when we had merely written her musical name?

Maud was nineteen, but as unlike the usual run of girls at that age as it was possible for her to be. Perfectly free from affectation, for she had no female friend to teach it her; without an ounce of vanity, she was as open, as pure, and as noble-minded as only a young girl of good birth brought up under such circumstances could be.

See her as she enters the breakfast room one November morning, clad in a dark morning dress of a deep, rich colour, that serves as a foil to her rich young beauty, her hair brushed from her fair white forehead, and her eyes sparkling with affection as she crosses to the fireplace, against which the tall form of her brother Chudleigh is leaning.

"Up already, Maud!" he exclaimed, taking her in his arms and lifting her up—unnecessarily—for a kiss. "I did not expect you for another half-hour."

"Well, don't look so disappointed, or I will go to bed again," she retorted, with a pout. "Is papa down yet?"

"Yes, in the library," replied Chudleigh; "I

have sent to tell him the coffee is on the table, but——"

"I will go," said Maud, and with a light step hurried from the room.

Chudleigh looked after her with a sigh and a sudden cloud across the brow, then resumed the old attitude—a somewhat despondent one—at the fire.

"Dear Maud, dear Maud," he muttered, "poor Maud—heigh-ho!"

In a few moments the door opened and the young girl re-entered with Sir Fielding Chichester leaning on her arm. In each hand was a book and in the breast of his waistcoat was a folded paper evidently thrust there in a moment of abstraction, and forgotten.

"Good morning, Chud, good morning," he exclaimed, in the musical voice that had always belonged to the Chichesters.

"Good morning, sir," said Chudleigh.

"Maud, my darling, what do you want with me?"

"Breakfast, you know, papa——"

"Ah, ah, dear me, yes," softly replied the baronet, "of course. How stupid of me. I had forgotten. Dear me, here are *Pliny's Letters* and the last *Essays of the Didactic Society*," and he looked at the books in his hand. "I—I brought them from the library. Excuse me a moment, Chudleigh, while I take them back," and he moved towards the door.

Maud rose from her seat hastily—she knew that once in the library again all remembrance of the breakfast would have vanished from Sir Fielding's mind.

"Let me take them, papa," she said, and with a kiss she took them from Sir Fielding's reluctant hands.

"Dear me, I had no idea it was snowing," he remarked, walking to the window. "What's the day of the month, Chud?"

"Twenty-sixth, sir," said Chudleigh.

"Twenty-sixth and the *Scientific Review* not

come yet," exclaimed Sir Fielding, shaking his head, and adding, softly, "very late—very late."

"The post has not come in yet," remarked Chudleigh. "I'm afraid Markham has some difficulty in driving."

Markham was the rural postman.

"Why, Chud, why?" asked the baronet, dreamily.

"The roads are so thick with snow—a foot deep round the Hollow."

"Ah, yes, the snow, dear me, dear me, the snow," murmured Sir Fielding, sinking into his chair by the fire. "Have you been out this morning?"

"Yes, sir," replied Chudleigh, "to see Giles. He is rather behindhand with his rent. New-born could do nothing with him, so I thought I'd walk over and see into it."

"Dear me," said the baronet, with perfect indifference, "and what does he say, Chud, what does he say?"

"The usual story. Everything gone wrong, crops short, the hay queer, mouth disease, and—oh, every mishap under the sun, of course. I was going to ask you what I am to do."

"My dear Chud, what is the use of asking me?" exclaimed the baronet, with mild surprise, "for you know I never interfere in any way with anything. I assure you I didn't even know that Giles was in arrears. I leave it to you, Chud, I leave it to you."

And the father wheeled his chair round towards the table with the air of having washed his hands of the subject.

The son sighed and his brows wrinkled as he looked at the serene face.

For a moment he was silent, then, drawing his chair towards the table, he balanced his knife thoughtfully, and with his face still troubled said:

"You know how sorry I always am to trouble you on business matters, sir, but I'm

afraid I must ask you to go over a few things
with me after breakfast."

"Yes, yes, after breakfast, dear Chud, after
breakfast," repeated Sir Fielding, catching
eagerly at the postponement.

The next . moment the door opened and
Maud re-entered with a letter-bag in her hand.

"Here's the post at last, Chud," she said.
Now, papa, let me see. Here are the papers,
your beloved *Quarterly*, the *Didactic Report*,
and a catalogue from Northeran's. Those for
you. Chud, here are your letters, and what
do you think ?—one from Aunt Mildred for
me."

Chudleigh looked up with a smile, but not
a very interested air, for he had already commenced the perusal of a pile of envelopes, and
the baronet took no notice whatever, for he
was lost in the contents of the *Quarterly*.

For a few minutes there was silence, broken
only by the trickling of the coffee into the cups
and the occasional play of Chudleigh's knife

and fork, but suddenly Maud looked up with a pleased smile upon her beautiful face, and said :

"Papa, Chud, what do you think ?"

Chud threw down his letters at once, and looked up all attention.

"Nothing. What do you ?"

"Aunt Mildred's coming here, and going to bring some one with her."

"Bring some one with her ? Whom ?" asked Chud.

"A companion," answered Maud. "Oh, how delightful. Listen, it's quite romantic :

"'You remember me telling you of a Captain Lawley, who has been staying in Paris for some months. He is dead, my dear. Is it not shocking ? He was shot in some wicked duel or other, and has left his daughter Carlotta, the beautiful girl I wrote to you about, you remember,—an orphan on the wide, wide world. Poor girl. She is so charming, so very charming, my dear Maud. You will be delighted with her.' Dear Aunt Mildred. She rather puzzled me, Chud, but a postscript explains it. 'We are coming over to England at once, as Paris is a painful locality, of course, for dear Carlotta. You have no idea how bravely she bears everything, for Captain Lawley left her penniless, and I had a hard struggle in persuading her from going into the world as a governess. Dreadful, is it not, my dear Maud? However, everything is settled now, and she is coming with me as my companion. We expect to reach London by the first of December, so that if you will kindly ask Chud to have the goodness to see to the cottage——' "

" First of December !" exclaimed Chudleigh, quickly. " Phew ! Just like Aunt Mildred. How on earth am I to get the cottage ready in a week ?" and he rose from the table and walked to the window thoughtfully.

He could see the little cottage which his Aunt Mildred had occupied since her husband,

Sir Wilford Gordon, had died; indeed, from where he stood he could scan the whole·village and most of the outlying houses — from the deserted Rectory, an old moss-grown mansion, tenantless for years, with a history mysterious and gloomy, to the great red-brick monstrosity which a self-made Manchester man had erected on the borders of the Chichester Park.

Lady Mildred's cottage, a pretty, rustic little box, just suited to her means, which were not very abundant, was about a quarter of an hour's walk from the Hall, and on a level with the dreary Rectory surrounded by its belt of thickly-planted trees, which seemed to overshadow the little church and all round it, like an army of giants with weird arms and clenched hands.

"I must ride over to Armsthorpe at once," said Chudleigh, returning to the table.

"Oh, yes, do, Chud," exclaimed Maud. "We must have the cottage ready for Aunt·Mildred.

Isn't it delightful, a companion, and such a charming one? I am sure I shall like her if she is anything half so nice as aunt describes her. Poor girl. Think, papa! her father killed in a duel and she left in a strange country without any money or friends excepting aunt. Oh, my heart is wrung for her! If she will let me, I will love her—that I will. Chud, you will make the cottage very nice, will you not?—very nice! Oh, Chud, let me come over to Armsthorpe with you; I can help you— I'm sure I can. I can choose different things, and——Oh, Chud, what is the matter?"

For Chud, who had been reading a letter in his hand, had suddenly started to his feet with an exclamation, whether of surprise or anxiety it was difficult to say.

"Eh, what's the matter, Chud?" asked Sir Fielding, glancing up from his *Quarterly*. "What's the matter?"

"N—nothing, sir," said Chudleigh, sitting down again, and placing the letter in his pocket. " Now, Maud, you want to go with me to Armsthorpe, so you shall ; go and get ready. I don't see how the cottage is to be prepared in time for Lady Mildred. Let me see—the twenty-sixth—no, I don't think it can be done."

"Then," said Maud eagerly, "let us have them here, papa."

" Of course, if your aunt will come, my dear," said Sir Fielding. " Of course, of course."

" I will write at once," said Maud. " Now, Chud, you need not be in such a hurry about the cottage—the longer the better. Another cup of coffee before I go, papa. Chud——? "

" No more, my darling," said Sir Fielding, and Chud had risen and walked to the window again.

So, holding the welcome letter in her hand, Maud ran from the room.

Chudleigh walked to the door, and held the handle.

Sir Fielding looked up, and actually shuffled in his chair.

"Well, Chud," he commenced, thinking it best to make a virtue of necessity, "you want to go over something with me, eh? I don't know what for, I am sure; for if it's anything of a muddle, it will be twenty times more muddled if I have anything to do with it. Figures, my dear Chud, were never my forte—never," and the baronet shook his head with mild emphasis.

His son came up to his chair, and leaning over him, put his hand upon his shoulder.

The baronet looked up with apprehensive astonishment, for Chudleigh was not usually demonstrative, and there was a meaning in his half-caressing grasp.

"What is it, Chud?" he said.

"Bad news, sir," replied Chudleigh gravely, taking the letter from his pocket and holding it out to his father. "Will you read that, sir?"

"No, no; you read—you tell me, Chud. Oh, from Norton and Read it seems by the look of it, and I never can read lawyers' writing. Tell me what is in it," said Sir Fielding, passing his white hand across his smooth forehead with a weary gesture.

Chudleigh opened the letter.

"There is not much to tell, sir," he said gravely. "Norton has received notice that Mr. Hassell intends foreclosing the mortgage."

Sir Fielding Chichester started, and his hand dropped from his forehead.

"What!" he said breathlessly. "Give me the letter."

Chudleigh gave it him.

"Norton writes as if there were no loophole left, and does not forget to remind you that the estate, having deteriorated, is not worth the sum advanced. I—I——"

Sir Fielding, who had not been listening to him, dropped the letter from his hand and staggered to his feet.

"Chud!" he said, drawing a long breath, "we are ruined!" and uttering a groan, he leant his arm on the mantelpiece and buried his face in it.

The son said nothing, but the twitching of the lip and sudden pallor proclaimed how great a struggle the calmness cost him.

There was a dead silence, in which the ticking of the antique bronze timepiece with its figure of the inexorable Father crushing down the minutes with a sweep of his deadly scythe, sounded harsh and foreboding.

Suddenly a burst of music floated into the room, and a girl's clear voice rang out joyfully from the room above in some simple ballad.

The father started as if he had been struck—the brother hid his face in his hands and groaned.

"Oh, Heaven—my Maud, my Maud!" breathed Sir Fielding, all the books in his heart turned out to make place for his darling. "My poor child! Chud, what shall we do?"

"Ay, what shall we do? that is the question," said Chudleigh, catching eagerly at the escape from the dread apathetic despair and drawing himself up to his full height. "Bear up, sir; all is not lost yet. Surely there is some one——"

Sir Fielding raised his head, startling Chudleigh at sight of his face, which looked ten years older than when he had seen it last.

"Some one! ay, but where? No, no, Chud; I have no friends now. I have been living out of the world for nearly twenty years. Once," and he walked to the window, Chudleigh following him—" once," raising his hand and pointing it for a second at the tall, crumbling chimneys of the Rectory, "there would have been refuge, for no Durant ever closed his hand against a Chichester, nor a Chichester ever denied a Durant. But," and he sighed with a world of mournfulness, "where is a Durant now? No,

Chudleigh, that was our only chance ; but you know how utterly that is lost to us."

And once more the baronet, gazing at the deserted house, sighed wearily and with utter hopelessness.

CHAPTER II.

"Grace was in all her steps, heaven in her eye,
In every gesture dignity and love."—MILTON.

THE first of December had arrived, and with it Lady Mildred, covered in furs, and accompanied by her friend and companion, Carlotta Lawley.

Chudleigh had been compelled to go to town the preceding day to see the family solicitor, and had not returned when her ladyship arrived, so that Sir Fielding and Maud did the honours of the house—Maud with some little shyness and reserve, for Miss Lawley had taken her by surprise. She had expected to see a beautiful and accomplished girl from her aunt's purposely obscure description, but the portrait her imagination had drawn fell so far short of the reality, that she was startled and surprised.

To say that Carlotta Lawley was beautiful was to assert but little. She was more proud and more bewitching than charming. Taller than Maud, a brilliant brunette, with dark, piercing eyes that shone like a jewel, or a gipsy's—a graceful form, almost queenly in its bearing, and a mouth that rivalled Cleopatra's in its coral-like curves and fulness—she was indeed what the best Parisian judges of woman's looks had called her—superb.

Beside Maud's fresh, fair loveliness her beauty shone to its greatest advantage, and Sir Fielding, who came from his dream-world with all the Chichester courtliness to welcome her, muttered a half audible note of admiration, which it was well for Carlotta's vanity did not reach her ear.

She was very quiet—naturally, thought Maud —but expressed her admiration of the grand old house with such fervour as to win Sir Fielding's and Maud's love immediately.

Said Maud, stopping before an open door through which a small sitting-room could be seen :

"These rooms are Chudleigh's. Oh, I forgot to tell you," she exclaimed, in answer to the look of interrogation on Carlotta's face. "Chudleigh is my brother. He is so good—so kind. We all of us lean on him. Papa is—is very busy in the library, you know, always, and everything is left to Chud. And everything fares well too. Oh, you must like Chudleigh."

"I am sure I shall if he resembles you in the slightest," murmured Carlotta.

"He went to London on business yesterday, but he will be back to dinner, I hope. You must let him take you all over the Hall—I mean in the closed-up rooms you know. He can tell you the history of every room."

"If he will take so much trouble, I shall only be too grateful," said Carlotta. "I am fond of old houses and their histories."

"And now you must come and see my room,"

she said, winding her arm round her new friend's waist, and leading her into the little rose-coloured boudoir and bed-chamber, which was honoured by the title of " Miss Maud's." " Do you like them ? If you do, you shall have them while you stay—and I wish that may be for ever."

" Do you ? " said Carlotta, leaning down with a sudden moisture in her dark eyes, her voice ringing tremulously musical—more musical than Maud had ever heard or thought it possible for a voice to be. " So do I ! How very kind you are ! You must forgive me if I seem somewhat cold ; until I knew Lady Mildred I never experienced such goodness."

And the lips quivered slightly, although the eyes lit up with a mournful smile.

Maud drew her closer to her.

" You must not say such things ; I am not kind. It seems so ridiculous to hear you say that to me." And she laughed merrily as she glanced at the grand beauty of the other, against which she looked so fresh and childlike.

" It's you who must be good to me. You will try and love me, won't you? I love you already."

Again the dark eyes filled with tears, but the lips said nothing as she stooped to kiss her.

" And now you must rest after your journey. See, I will make up the fire and cover you up with these furs. Then, while I go and see whether Aunt Mildred is comfortable, you can have a quiet sleep."

Carlotta Lawley laughed a low, musical laugh.

" Sleep!" she said. " I could not. I am not tired. You do not know how much I have travelled in my short life, or you would not think me worn out by a short trip from Paris. I once journeyed from Siberia, night and day, and had but six hours' sleep the whole time."

Maud gazed at her with something approaching awe.

"Siberia! Oh, dear me! what a great deal you will have to tell me!" she said, with a quiet delight, but added suddenly, "but perhaps you won't tell me?"

"Yes, I will tell you everything," replied Carlotta, "nearly everything."

Meanwhile Lady Mildred—a good-natured lady, loved and respected by all, who bore about her the Chichester characteristics in features and manner—was narrating to her brother the history—or rather what little she knew of it—of Carlotta and her father, Captain Lawley.

Womanlike, she of course commenced the conversation by asking Sir Fielding what he thought of her new companion.

"She is majestic," he said, "Oriental in her beauty. What a woman her mother must have been! Who was she?"

"No one knows," said Lady Mildred. "Captain Lawley had been a widower for years, so it is said. He was a strange man, Fielding such a very strange man — very handsome. Carlotta has her father's eyes, and his hair too."

" What was he ? " said Sir Fielding.

" Ah, that too no one knows. He had travelled a great deal. He had been to—oh, I don't know where—every country you can mention. He could speak every language on the face of the earth, I think. I have heard him scold an Arab who used to bring us flowers in Paris in pure Arabic."

" Eh, how do you know it was pure ? " asked Sir Fielding, with a quiet smile, not half attending to her.

" Oh—ahem !—how absurd, Fielding ! How do I know it was pure ? Why, how could the man have understood him if it hadn't been ? Ah, he was a strange character ! So gentlemanly, he looked a lord ; but—well, very wild, I think. There were stories about a Russian princess, an escapade at court, and a dismissal ; but people will talk, you know, and tell such stories too. Anyway, everybody said that something had happened in some court or other, and that Captain Lawley was a ruined man. I never will believe he was an adventurer. No one who could bow as he did could be an adventurer."

"Hem!" said Sir Fielding. "And what about the duel?"

"Ah, was not that sad?" said Lady Mildred, throwing up her hands. "Ah, it was dreadful! I don't know what it was about—never could find out. Some said that it was a gambling affair; but there again, you see, reports are so untrue. Poor Captain Lawley! I am sure I was as grieved as if he'd been my own brother when they told me that he was shot through the breast—through the heart, Fielding—think of that!"

"And this poor girl is utterly penniless," said Sir Fielding, "eh, utterly penniless, didn't you say?"

"Hasn't a penny in the world. Shocking, is it not, with such doubtful antecedents and no fortune? Poor Carlotta!"

Then the conversation ended by Sir Fielding getting up in an abstracted manner and walking dreamily out of the room, of course in the direction of the library. Lady Mildred, who was too used to her brother's queer ways to be offended, then sought her dressing-room.

Two hours afterwards the four met in the oaken dining-room.

Chudleigh had not arrived, and Sir Fielding, as he stood at the head of the table, pulled out his watch with an anxious look.

"Chudleigh is late," he said. "Had he any commission from you, Maud?"

"No," said Maud, from where she was sitting beside Carlotta, who was dressed in deep mourning, that set off her clear skin to perfection. "No; he said he should not have time to do more than buy some books for you at Chester's, papa."

"Ah, ah," said Sir Fielding, sighing, "I'm afraid he hasn't been able to get the books. They were very scarce. An old copy of

'Marcus Aurelius' and a marginal 'Ovid,' my dear Miss Lawley, a marginal 'Ovid!'"

"That must be very scarce," said Carlotta quietly. "I have only seen one, and that was at Lorenzo Bardolphus's."

"Eh," exclaimed Sir Fielding eagerly. "Have you been over Lorenzo's library?"

"Yes," she said simply. "I have spent days there."

"Dear me, dear me," said Sir Fielding, forgetting the soup which had just been brought in, and Lady Mildred's plate which was being held beside him.

"I envy you, I envy you. Lorenzo Bardolphus's library, and you saw the 'Ovid!' Perhaps you saw that old tractate of Gregory's. I heard he had a copy."

"My dear Carlotta, don't say a word more," interrupted Lady Mildred, "or I shall never get any soup."

Maud laughed.

"Soup! Dear me, yes," said Sir Fielding.

" You will tell me about Lorenzo's after dinner, will you not, Miss Lawley? After dinner! Yes, yes."

Before Carlotta's " Yes " had died upon her lips, the door opened, and Chudleigh entered, He started at seeing the beautiful girl at his sister's side ; for, like every one else, her loveliness took him by surprise. And she, Carlotta, was, on her part, somewhat startled ; for, from Maud's description, she had drawn for herself the picture of a little, undersized man, rather poor-looking, very business-like, and wholly unprepossessing, whereas Chudleigh Chichester, as he stood in evening dress, with the glow of exercise upon his handsome face, looked none of these.

Sir Fielding looked up anxiously, trying to read, if he could, his son's tidings from his face. Then, discovering nothing, and smothering a sigh, he introduced him to Carlotta, Maud making room for her brother between them.

D

"I didn't hear you come in, Chud," said Sir Fielding.

"I walked up the avenue," said Chud. Then, turning to Carlotta, he added, "You have had a cold and wearisome journey?"

"A little," she said, answering the kindly regard of his great, honest eyes, in which still lingered a touch of his first admiring surprise— "a little; we were well wrapped up, were we not, Lady Mildred?"

"Yes, my dear," said Lady Mildred, "and well taken care of too; for a gentleman, very good-looking, was exceedingly attentive, and insisted on converting Carlotta and myself into respectable mummies with waterproofs and shawls, besides bringing us hot soup and coffee every five minutes. Of course Martha was too ill to move."

Martha was Lady Mildred's maid.

"A right courteous gentleman. Do you know his name?"

"We did hear it, but I have forgotten it,"

said her ladyship. "Do you remember, Carlotta?"

"No, I do not. I heard some one address him as the Honourable Mr. something, and that was all. He was very kind."

Chudleigh looked round from his soup at the pale, grand face, and wondered how under the circumstances any one could be otherwise.

"Let me send you some snipe, Miss Lawley," said Sir Fielding, glancing at her empty plate.

But she declined.

"You are eating nothing," said Maud, with loving reproach.

"You are tired," said Chudleigh; "let me give you some wine," and he poured out a glass of port.

"I do not wonder at her being worn out. She would not lie down even for half an hour, aunt. It was very wrong, was it not?" said Maud.

"Carlotta is very young," said Lady Mildred,

"and can afford to be extravagant with her energy. When she gets to my age——"

"My dear Mildred," expostulated Sir Fielding, in so comically courteous a tone that all laughed, even Carlotta; and Chudleigh, in whose ears her voice had been ringing since she had first spoken, drank in the low, rippling laughter as one listening to some marvellous music.

A spell seemed to fall over him when she spoke, and towards the close of the dinner he was startled to find himself setting traps to catch her speech, and listening with rapt attention to her low replies.

"Now Chud and I will have one little bottle," said Sir Fielding, "and then join you in the drawing-room. I must send you to bed early to-night, Miss Lawley, but after to-day you shall do as you like. Chichester Hall is Liberty Hall—eh, Aunt Mildred? Liberty Hall, eh?" and the old baronet rubbed his white hands agreeably. "Now, Chud, what of the night?"

he said, anxiously, as soon as the door had closed on the ladies, and the old butler had disappeared.

" Black, sir," he said. " Norton says that for the present nothing can be done ; but he is keeping a careful look-out for a fresh mortgagee, although he fears the estate must be sold."

Sir Fielding groaned.

" My poor Chud!" he said. " This is hard for you—very hard."

Chudleigh smiled bravely.

" I can bear it, sir," he said ; then, with a touch of pride : " We Chichesters, sir, are not used to give in easily. I am not an idiot, I hope, and can make my way. As for Maud— there is her mother's money."

" A mere pittance, Chud, a mere pittance," said Sir Fielding, in a dry voice."

" Five hundred a year, sir," replied Chud, suppressing a sigh and speaking cheerily. " Five hundred a year is not to be lamented over."

Sir Fielding sighed deeply, and his eyes filled with tears.

"Maud Chichester with five hundred a year, and the heir to Chichester Hall working for his daily bread!" he breathed.

A million others, more deserving men, do, sir," said Chudleigh, eagerly, his face flushing and his hand unconsciously clasping the thin claret glass until the stem snapped. Then he continued, more quietly and with great feeling: "Think of yourself, sir; you will suffer most. You are not young, not strong, sir, as we are. Your books——"

Sir Fielding winced.

"Think of myself," he said, in a tone of self-reproach and with a twitching of the lips. "I have been thinking of myself too long, Chud. I might have repaired the hole in the wall if I had buckled to it in earnest. The estate is a large one, and, like a mine, would pay well if it were properly worked. I might at least have made the old Hall safe for you, Chud; but I have been living a dream-life all these years, shut up like an anchorite between four walls of books—and, oh, Chud, Chud! though I know it is selfish, I feel the coming loss of my books almost as much as anything."

And the poor man, so great a student of the great past, so ignorant a novice of the present, bent his face in his hands and groaned again.

Chudleigh's eyes burnt and he felt choking, but he looked positively stern as, struggling with might and main to suppress his emotion, he said :

" Bear up, sir, for God's sake, bear up. We will save the books at all cost. Come, sir, to the drawing-room. Of course the women must not know a word of this."

" Not a word," said Sir Fielding, taking the strong arm held out to him, and father and son walked into the drawing-room.

CHAPTER III.

"There stands the house in solemn gloom,
Black as the night and dismal as the tomb."

"MAUD, I am trying to persuade Miss Lawley to accompany me to the village. It is bright over head, crisp under foot, and not too cold. I have offered to play showman to all the dead, brick-and-mortar lions, and see that she does not take cold; but still she hesitates. Can you throw in a word to weigh down the balance?"

So said Chudleigh, leaning against the balustrade in the great hall, clad in rich garments of seal and Cheviot, and as he spoke he looked up smilingly to where Maud was standing, then at Carlotta, who, book in hand, stood at the open door of the drawing-room.

"Liberty Hall, Liberty Hall," said Maud, her soft, bright face lit up with a smile. "You can trust yourself to his guidance, Carlotta, if you care to go. He is very safe, and will not let you slip."

"I am not afraid of slipping," replied Carlotta, quietly; "but," she continued, with a smile, "shall I not be troubling you?"

"I have won," said Chudleigh, eagerly. "If that is your only objection you can go and get your bonnet at once. But—don't let me take you away from your book by force," he said, suddenly, a doubt seizing him whether she really cared to go or not.

"I should like to go very much, if I should not trouble you."

So they went, walking side by side down the avenue and across the park into the clear, frost-bound road that led to the village.

"Now for the lions," said Chudleigh. "You see that red house on the hill there? Guess what it is."

"I cannot," she said. "It is very ugly. The workhouse."

Chudleigh laughed.

"Oh, capital," he said, enjoyingly. "I must tell that to Sir Fielding. He will love you to the end of his days. That is Gregson's Folly, built by a Manchester millionaire, named Gregson. His grounds border upon the park; but we see very little of the family, as my father has taken umbrage at the close proximity of Gregson's palatial dwelling-place."

"A millionaire?" said Carlotta, gazing, as it seemed to her companion, with sudden interest at the ugly monstrosity.

"Ay, a millionaire," said Chudleigh, with a touch of sadness in his deep voice. "It is a grand title, is it not?"

"Yes," she said, and, to his surprise, a deep gravity came into her voice and eyes. "Yes; wealth is the grandest thing in this world."

For a moment he was too astonished to reply. He found it difficult to believe that the sweet,

pure lips could have uttered such an assertion;
then he said, earnestly:

"I do not think so. And—you will pardon
me—I am astonished to hear you say so. Ah!
you were sarcastic?"

"No, I was not," she said, simply. "You
have never been acquainted with poverty; I
have. A lion in a story book and face to face
in a huge forest are two different things."

He looked at her, and would have replied,
but a something about her lips stopped him.

"Has he any children?" 'she said.

"Yes, two daughters and a son," said Chudleigh. "We don't know much of them, because
Sir Fielding will not visit them. I meet the
Gregsons, father and son, in parochial affairs
occasionally, and Maud is on speaking terms
with the ladies. Indeed, she rather likes them,
and would have been glad to have accepted
their invitations, but my father is stern, and
his decrees are as unalterable as were those of
the Medes and Persians."

"There is the barrier of Caste betwixt the Hall and the Folly," said Carlotta, dreamily.

"That is it," said Chudleigh, with a smile. "But it is a barrier not of my building, remember."

"That is a pretty cottage," said Carlotta, as they entered a little lane, whose frosted hedges and bare, thick-boughed trees gave promise of a verdant avenue in summer-tide.

"You like it?" he said, eagerly. "That is your future home!"

"Lady Mildred's!" she said, the colour rising to her face.

"Yes," he said. "It is very beautiful in the summer. The river runs at the back, an orchard stands at its side, and there is a croquet lawn unrivalled in the county."

"You have pictured an Eden," she said, smiling.

"It is—at least to me," he said. "I spend —that is to say, I used to spend," he put in quickly, and the girl flushed slightly at the

addendum, "most of my time here. There is
a little boathouse at the end of the garden,
where many treasures of mine in the shape of
angling, shooting, and skating lie hidden. Are
you fond of boating?"

"I don't know what to answer," she said.
"My experience of boating is un-English. I
only know the gondola of Venice."

"Venice!" said Chudleigh. "You have
added another story to the edifice of envy.
I do envy you. You seem to have travelled
all over the globe."

"You would not," she said, gravely, "if you
knew all. What is that little Gothic place
there?"

"Our curate's; that is the steeple of the old
church you see in the hollow there. We have
no rector, you know—or, rather, of course you
don't. The curate holds a sort of perpetual
appointment. He's a very capital little fellow,
does his work well, and is respected and liked
from one end of the parish to the other. His

ıme is Hawes—Stephen Hawes. There he is,"
ıd Chudleigh raised his hat as a short, fair-
ıired young man, dressed in the usual eccle-
astical long coat and high waistcoat, emerged
ɔm the doorway of a cottage.

Then they walked on towards a dark-looking
ece of woodland until they reached a broken
oss-eaten gate which barred a path weed-
ɔwn and untrodden.

Holding it open for Carlotta, Chudleigh
ıid :

"We are going to the old Rectory."

"A rectory here!" she said ; "how deserted
ıd unclerical it looks."

Chudleigh did not reply, and they traversed
long, winding path, as solitary and overgrown
ı the piece at the gate, for some distance, the
ees growing thicker and more wild-looking,
hen a sudden turn brought them to a large
ṭuare that had once been a lawn, but was
ɔw nothing but a wilderness of long rank
·ass, and Carlotta, looking up, saw facing her

a huge, straggling mansion of ancient architecture, and bearing on its every side some sign of decay and neglect. Its time-eaten walls, down which the damp had drawn long green wrinkles, its black, dust-obscured windows, broken gables, and rotting stonework filled her with nameless awe and dread, and her voice insensibly quivered and grew hushed as she said :

"And this is the Rectory?"

"Yes, this is the Rectory," replied Chudleigh, with slow gravity. "It is a grand old ruin, is it not?"

"Yes, grand and awful," she replied, dreamily, gazing at the forsaken pile with thoughtful eyes.

"You could scarcely imagine this house alight and alive with warmth and colour, wealth and prosperity, only twelve years back, can you?"

"No," she said, simply, "the windows look as if no human face had ever gazed through them, the steps as if they had never been trodden upon, and this grass plot I cannot imagine anything but the soul-stirring piece of wilderness it is."

"And yet only twelve years back the Rectory, for life and merriment, could outshine any house in the county. There is a history attached to it. Would you like to hear an outline while we walk round?"

"I am eager to hear anything respecting it," she said, and her large dark eyes lit up curiously.

"Once upon a time, then, you must know that the Durants—singular name, isn't it?—strangers always call it 'Durrant'—it is Durant, the 'Du' long—were amongst the mightiest people of this part of the land. They were of very ancient lineage, but without titles, for they invariably refused them, of enormous wealth, and great popularity. The land you see round this deserted place had belonged to them as long as any one could remember, how long no one could find out, though many an antiquary had pored over parchment and

black letter in his endeavour to do so. We
Chichesters, though priding ourselves on our
old name, are mushrooms compared to the
Durants. No, I was wrong in saying that
they had no title, for they always had one in
the family, and that was Reverend. The son,
generally the eldest in each generation, held
the living of Grassmere, and since the old
church has been built it has owned no rector-
ship save that of Durant. Don't be alarmed ;
I am not going to take you back to the first
Durant and downward, with a history attached
to each. I am only going to tell you how
this old place came to be deserted.

"You must know, then, that the present
owner is a certain Maurice Durant, who disappeared twelve years ago, and has never been
heard of since. His father, Gerald Durant, was
a schoolfellow and firm friend of my father,
though totally unlike him, having no taste for
books or study, and being rather given to hard
riding, hard drinking, and fast spending. Still,

E

however, they were great friends, and I don't believe that Sir Fielding has ever known another man to whom he could give the same confidence.

"Gerald Durant married ten years before my father and had one son, this Maurice mentioned, of whom he was worthily proud. His love for him was a passion partaking of the fearful in its intensity, so they say, and 'Gerald's Boy' was a by-word in the county. Nothing was good enough for him. No extravagance was sufficiently prodigal to meet his wishes. Nothing Maurice desired, if it was on earth and procurable at any cost, did his father deny him. The result you can imagine. Maurice grew into manhood with the pride of a king and the hauteur of a Spanish hidalgo. He was sent to college, and there, to the almost unutterable delight of his father, he took honours and holy orders. He was very clever, could paint and play—indeed, had taken a Bac. Mus. degree with the other honours. He

came of age. The whole village was decorated. Twelve oxen were roasted whole. A
flock of sheep and several thousand pounds
were given to the poor, and a grand ball, dis-
tinguished by a princely magnificence, was held
at the Hall, at which gathered the *élite* of the
county and a host of the best blood from the
Court, all in honour of Maurice. Then came
the time when he grew restless. He must
travel.

"Gerald Durant, for the first time in his life,
gave a reluctant consent, but still consent. A
tutor and companion was obtained, and the
parting, which nearly broke the old man's heart,
took place.

" Maurice started for the Continent. For six
months letters came from him with tolerable
regularity. At the end of that time they grew
few and far between. The father looked wan
and anxious—more wan and anxious when they
ceased altogether, and no messenger or inquiry
could discover the whereabouts or the track of

the missing son — for it had come to that. Maurice Durant had given his tutor and servants the slip one moonlight night in some German village, and had flown, leaving no sign behind.

"Then the father's heart grew harder. His hand was closed against the poor, and his house against his friends. He shut himself up in this dreary place, refused all offers of consolation and comfort, and waited for the end.

"It came.

"One bleak March night a horseman rode up the avenue along which we have just walked, and, dripping with the rain, his hair blown across his face by the wind, demanded to see Gerald Durant.

"He was refused admittance. It was Mr. Durant's order that no stranger should pass the threshold of the Rectory. The horseman thrust a letter into the servant's hand, and bade him bear it to his master, saying it contained tidings of his son. The servant took it to the dim, ghastly room, lined with faded tapestry and dusty books, in which the old man spent the few remaining days this side of eternity, and then retired. An hour afterwards, fancying he heard a noise, he returned, and found his master stretched across the table—dead. The contents of the letter no one ever knew, for all that remained of it was a little heap of ashes in the grate, and the horseman had vanished as suddenly and mysteriously as he had appeared.

"That is the history of the Rectory, as I have heard it a hundred times. Miss Lawley, you are quite pale, and, surely, not weeping? How thoughtless of me. I might have known that the cheerless place and the story would have affected you. Pray——"

And with self-reproachful eagerness he seized her arm.

"Forgive me, I am very foolish," she said; "but you told it too graphically. I could see the poor old man! And has he—Maurice, did you not say?—never been heard of?"

" Never," said Chudleigh, curtly, anxious to get away from the subject. " Now let me take you to see the church. No, stay, that is too dismal after this. We will walk round the village home and finish the lions another day."

CHAPTER IV.

Nothing is better, I well think,
　Than love ; the hidden well water
　Is not so delicate to drink.　　　SWINBURNE.

Oh, great one, some men love and are ashamed ;
　Some men are weary of the bonds of love :
Yea, and by some men lightly art thou blamed,
　That, from thy toils their life they cannot move,
　And 'mid the ranks of men their manhood prove.
　　*　　　*　　　*　　　*　　　*
Think then will it bring honour to thy head
　If folk say, " Everything aside he cast,
And to all fame and honour was he dead " ?
　　　　　　　　　　　　　　　MORRIS.

A WEEK passed, rapidly as it seemed to the inmates of the Hall, for to Sir Fielding there were seven days less of the short grace afforded him to meet the large sum required.

To his son, Chudleigh, the days had flown by with the speed happiness always lends time, for he was happy—happy with a strange inward joy, the source of which he could not discern, although he had only to search his own heart to unearth it immediately. So happy was he in those short December days, notwithstanding the cloud which hung over his fortunes, that he longed for them to last for ever.

As for Maud, rejoicing with all her heart in the acquisition of her new friend, she was more prodigal of her rippling laughter and sunny smiles than ever, and flitted through the old house with her arm wound round the waist of the beautiful Carlotta like a flash of sunlight leading the moon captive.

And Carlotta, whether she were happier than usual her face and manner did not chronicle. Always speaking in the soft-toned musical voice, always ready to exchange serene, loving glances with Maud, or a quiet smile for some pleasantry of Chudleigh's, she looked as if she were too used to change, pleasant or otherwise, to be affected by the sudden gleam of peace

and prosperity thrown across her path. Only
to Sir Fielding did her serenely calm bearing
ever vary ; to him her manner was inexpressibly
soft and tender. Her attention was absorbed
immediately by him if he spoke to her; she
would listen to his rambling, old-lore talk with
her dark eyes fixed on his face, wearing an
expression which Chudleigh would have given
a world, had he possessed it, to find in them
when she looked his way. For, try as he would
to ignore the fact, Chudleigh's heart was slipping away from him fast, his knees were bending
to the dark, queen-like form with the adoration
of love.

He struggled against it manfully, for he read
no encouragement in Carlotta's eyes, but the
strange thrill at her chance touch, and the
buoyant feeling of happiness in her presence,
and the joyous echo of his heart to her low
musical laugh grew hour by hour.

During the week Chudleigh had fulfilled his
promise, and finished the lions for Carlotta, but

after that first day when he told the story of the
the Rectory they were always accompanied by
Maud.

Fond as he was of his sister, he could have
spared her presence in these winter walks and
gallops, but some chance word of Carlotta
always brought Maud with them, and Chud's
sensitiveness, quickened by the sharp point of
Cupid's dart, perceived that Carlotta purposely
planned against another *tête-à-tête* with him, and
for a little time the idea gave a certain reserve
and coldness to his manner, but the ice melted
beneath the calm serenity of Carlotta's smile,
and before three days had passed he was as
much in bondage as ever.

Once or twice in the course of conversation
Carlotta let fall some incident or other of her
strange life, but it was only when off her guard
as it seemed, and each flash of confidence was
followed by a tightening of the lip and a sudden
marked reserve, which only served to deepen
the mystery in which her life seemed wrapped.

On the eighth day of their sojourn at the Hall, Chudleigh walked into the drawing-room where Lady Mildred, Carlotta and Maud were sitting, and passing up to her ladyship's arm-chair beside the fire, said :

" I have just seen Chaffer, the decorator. He tells me the cottage is quite finished."

" Eh ?" said Lady Mildred, waking from a pleasant dream of a game at whist she was playing with a good hand and half-crown points. "What do you say, my dear Chud? The cottage finished ? Carlotta, do you hear ? We must think of packing."

Chudleigh tried to laugh with polite indiffer-ence, but there was an eagerness in his voice he could not hide.

" Packing !—nonsense, aunt ! That the cottage is finished is no reason why you should fly from the Hall like a caged pigeon suddenly released. Besides, I could not think of allowing you to go for another"—week he was going to say, but in for a penny in for a pound—" month——"

"Nonsense, Chud!" interrupted Lady Mildred, "another month. Long enough to dry a cathedral. Besides, the cottage has only been whitewashed and repapered, or something of that sort, has it not?"

"Oh, lots of things; it's very damp indeed, very damp," said Chudleigh, earnestly. "You mustn't think of going for some weeks at least."

"Ah, but I want to get settled, Chud. Think how long I have been away, gadding about. Have some fires lit all over the house, and—and do anything of that sort you can think of, Chud, there is a dear boy, so that we may get into our little nest—Carlotta and I—in three or four days."

"You are in a great hurry to leave the Hall, aunt," said Chudleigh, with a slight frown, then, walking over to where Maud and Carlotta sat leaning over some views of Italy, he added, "I hope Miss Lawley is not so anxious to fly from us—at least, she will not declare her eagerness so openly."

She looked up with a smile at his anxious yet smiling face.

"You know I am not," she said. "I should be very sorry to go but that we shall not be far away, you know. We can see the north turret from the cottage."

"Oh, you must not go yet," broke in Maud, eagerly. "What should I do without you? and what would papa? If you go there will be no one to talk to him about his authors, or find quotations in his books. Oh, aunt, you must not go. It will be so lonely when you are gone, will it not, Chud?"

Chud said nothing, perhaps he did not hear from where he stood beside the fire, looking into the glowing coals.

"Say you will stay another fortnight," continued Maud, going over to her aunt and kissing her. "Be a good auntie, and let me have Carlotta a little longer."

"Carlotta can stay, my dear, if she likes," said Lady Mildred, graciously.

Chudleigh looked up quickly.

"Will you stay?" he said, eagerly.

She shook her head.

"No, thank you very much. If Lady Mildred will let me, I will accompany her," she said, almost coldly, after a minute's pause, lifting her eyes for one instant to his face. "No, I think I will go with Lady Mildred."

Chudleigh said nothing more. Perhaps the remembrance that he could see the cottage from the north turret at any time he liked to mount it was consolation enough to keep him silent.

In a week's time they had gone, and the Hall seemed strangely still and solemn without Lady Mildred's quick, cheerful chatter and Carlotta's low-toned voice.

Chudleigh had gone over with them in the carriage, and, waiting barely long enough to receive his aunt's thanks for the way in which the cottage was decorated, and Carlotta's few quiet words in admiration of the drawing-room, returned to the Hall with a nameless void in his heart and a great feeling of *ennui.*

Maud was in her boudoir, and, hearing him pass on his way to his own room, she called him.

"Back already, Chud, dear?" she said as he came behind her chair and stooped to kiss her. "I did not expect you back to dinner, and was thinking how lonely I should feel with only quiet papa and Simmons, the butler, to keep me company. Why didn't you stay, Chud?"

"Why didn't I?" said Chud. "Why should I? It is not likely they would ask me on the very first day of their taking possession. I should have been in the way—a nuisance."

"A dear old nuisance," breathed Maud, caressing his hand. "What do you think of Carlotta? Is she not beautiful, grandly beautiful?"

"Yes," said Chudleigh, staring at the fire.

"And so clever. She knows all about the

old books and the new ones too, which papa
is so fond of, and has travelled so very much.
My poor geography does not go half so far
as Carlotta has been. Yet, poor thing, while
I envy her I cannot help pitying her at the
same time, can you, Chud? She seems so
unnaturally quiet, so solemnly calm, and her
smile, though it is so beautiful, is so sorrowful
and sad sometimes. Do you know, Chud, I
think Carlotta has not found life very pleasant
up to this time. She so seldom speaks of her
father, never of herself, and seems to shun the
past so carefully. Did you notice that, Chud?"

"Yes," said Chud again.

Maud looked up.

"Are you listening, brother mine? I don't
believe you heard or understood a word of
what I have been saying."

"Yes, I have, little one," said Chud. "I
was thinking."

"What of?" said Maud. "Those horrible
books and accounts the steward is always

bothering you about, I suppose. Poor Chud, they are worrying you into wrinkles!"

She laughed sweetly as she stroked his strong hand with her tiny soft ones.

He had not been thinking of them, but her words brought them to his mind and deepened the shadow across his forehead.

What if he did love? No, no; it could not be. He was poor. He had his way to fight, and could not drop his sword or unbuckle his armour to woo and wed a portionless girl, the daughter of a man whom the world called an adventurer, be she as queenly as Cleopatra and as beautiful as the first mother, Eve.

"We shall have a storm," he said, stretching his great limbs into an upright position. "How much longer are you going to toast your toes, miss? I must go and dress."

F

CHAPTER V.

Behold your house is left unto you desolate.

THE storm prophesied by Chudleigh had come, dashing the sleet against the windows of the library, and causing Sir Fielding to look up from his book with a start, rattling through the avenue of chestnuts as if it meant to strip the trees of their very branches, and sweeping across the moor, and amidst the belt of oaks round the deserted Rectory, till they bent beneath the bitter blast, and moaned like living creatures writhing beneath a scourge.

It would seem impossible for a human being to stand against the furious drenching of the icy sleet, yet the dark figure of a man, closely wrapped in a black cloak of foreign make and shape, bent its head against the downpour, and, struggling like a wrecking ship in the deep troughs of a heavy sea, literally fought its way across the moor in the direction of the wood.

Sometimes when the wind paused to gain fresh strength and fury, and the blinding sleet lifted and lightened for a moment, the man quickened his pace like one well accustomed to wrestle with the elements, and used the respite to good purpose, tightening his cloak around him, then, bending his head lower when the wind rose again, he relapsed into the old attitude of stolid determination.

It was a grand sight to witness the tall, massive frame capped by a well-formed head, round which a wealth of thick black hair was blown with each gust of the wind; the dark face lit up by large, piercing, sadly resolute eyes, and ennobled by a handsome though sternly set mouth, contesting inch by inch the desolate path with the furious elements.

For an hour the struggle lasted, the wayfarer progressing slowly but surely towards the friendly haven of the dark oaks looming in the distance : and relaxing his sturdy attitude not one whit, nor resting a moment till he had reached the rickety gate—which had been torn from its rusted hinges, and lay a perfect wreck upon the ground—and stood panting, but triumphant, beneath the leafless branches of a huge old oak.

Then loosening his coat, he raised his travelling cap, and sweeping his scattered hair from off his wet forehead, exclaimed :

"Whew! a tough fight. England, I left thee in a storm, thy thunders hurling menace at my back, and I return to find thee no more courteous, but prepared to sweep me from thy face with ice and sleet!"

Then he leaned against the tree, and, folding his arms, looked moodily round upon what little he could see of the desolation around.

"A wreck!" he muttered, moodily. "A wreck! God forsaken and man forsaken! Ah, old trees! what have you and I suffered since last you looked down upon me? We both bear traces of it too. You are black and gnarled, and I—bah!—who says the Wandering Jew lives but in fable? The old house must be almost within sight. Strange that my heart leaps at the thought of seeing it! I fancied there was scarce enough blood left in me to leap at anything! But the old house—the old house!"

Then he relapsed into silence for a moment, his face growing darker and his eyes blacker as he gazed moodily at the sodden ground; but suddenly his self-communing commenced again, abruptly, almost fiercely.

"Why should I see it? What good can it do thee, thou lost sheep, to stare at the old homestead? What good, say I?—rather what amount of evil? A happy past is best forgot, it makes the bitter present more galling to the

mind. Bah! does the air of England breed
sentiment, or has the storm scattered the little
brains I had ?"

And, shaking himself till the wet flew from
his cloak in a shower of glistening drops, he
emerged from the shelter of the tree and strode
up the path which led to the front of the
desolate mansion.

Then, looking up at its windows re-echoing
the storm, his face grew white, and his hands,
large and sinewy, clenched under his cloak
across his heart, vainly trying to keep down
the storm raging within, that threatened to burst
forth in unison with the storm without.

For a moment he stood motionless as a
statue, then drawing a deep breath of pain he
groaned between his clenched teeth :—

"'Behold, your house is left unto you desolate !' "

And, muttering this twice, thrice, a score of
times, he stood, exposed to the pitiless sleet and
the fury of the wind, gazing at the ruined house

as if he were indeed the senseless stone he re-
sembled.

*　　*　　*　　*　　*　　*

When the storm commenced Maud was in
the drawing-room, idly fingering the keys of
the grand piano, occasionally breaking away
from her thoughts sufficiently to play a scrap
from one of the operas.

Once she commenced singing an old English
ballad which her father had dug up from some
forgotten collection, but the wind played so
·discordant an accompaniment to the soft sad
words, that she ceased, and half determined to
go in search of Chud, who was writing a letter
in his own room ; but, struggling against her
weakness, she sat still to listen to the rattling
sleet, and touching the keys restlessly, commenced Gounod's " Ave Maria," but at the first
bar of that melody—surely the most sublime
of devotional music—she succeeded in forgetting
the storm, and, half closing her eyes, lost herself in the subtle wailing of the music, which

rang through the room like a living friend bringing consolation and assurance.

As she played, the tall, dark figure, which but a little time since stood gazing at the deserted Rectory, was rooted, bare-headed, outside the window, its face sunk upon its breast and its hands clasped in front of it.

With the last note throbbing, dying through the air, Maud rose, and, the glamour of the music still over her, seated herself in a low chair by the fire, and there, lulled by the storm and the dead red of the coals, she fell asleep, her beautiful face lit up with the smile that only the pure and childlike at heart can wear.

How long she slept she knew not, but a slight noise awakened her, and, looking up with a start, she saw the dark figure of a man standing in the room looking at her.

With a low cry of alarm she rose from the chair.

The stranger lifted his head with a grave smile, such that reassured her even before his lips opened, and, in a voice whose noble gentleness charmed all her fear away, said :

"Madam, be not afraid ; I am not so harmful as my appearance may proclaim me. For this intrusion I crave with painful humility your forgiveness. It was not intentional ; I sought Sir Fielding Chichester. The night is dark and the storm confusing, and I, a stranger, missed the path. Nay, rather, your music drew me from it. By some chance a side door had been blown open by the wind ; I entered— wrongly, I admit with sorrow—and, meeting no one, found my way here, when I would rather have perished in the storm than entered if I have caused you one second's uneasiness."

Pouring out this strange confession in a voice almost tremulous in its musical softness, with a slightly foreign accent that lent it an additional charm, and expressing with a slight gesture the most profound yet eager humility, he bent low before her.

"I—I am not frightened," said Maud, her

aze riveted on the face and form that were
oble and kingly notwithstanding their expres-
ion of profound respect. " I will call my father.
Vill you be seated ?" and, still unable to re-
1ove her eyes from him, she walked towards
he door.

With a gesture he declined a seat, and cross-
ng to the fire, leaning one arm upon the carved
nantel, the firelight making a ruddy background
o his stalwart form, looked towards the door
nd waited.

In a few minutes it opened, and Sir Fielding
ntered, and advancing towards the stranger
aid, in his mild, dreamy voice :

" You wish to see me ?"

The stranger fixed his dark eyes upon the
)ale, smooth face for a moment, seemingly
ibsorbed in contemplation, then, waking as it
vere with a start, replied, in a voice from which
ill the tenderness had gone—

" Do you wish to see me, Sir Fielding Chi-
:hester ?"

The old man started with an exclamation, then, going close up to the speaker and scanning his features anxiously, exclaimed, as his face lit up with the light of recognition:

"Maurice Durant!"

The son of Gerald Durant, for it was he, nodded.

"Yes, Maurice Durant. You are surprised, Sir Fielding, yet not so much as I, for a week since I had as little thought of seeing your Chichester Hall as Heaven."

"Thank God!—thank God!" exclaimed Sir Fielding, grasping the outstretched hand, and wringing it with his feeble one. "Oh, Maurice, Maurice! we all thought you were dead."

"Heaven has not proved so kind," muttered Maurice Durant.

"We never expected to see you again. And you have come back to us as suddenly as— as——"

"Why do you hesitate?" said Maurice, frowning. "Yes. A week since I was sleeping in a peasant's hut beside an Alpine ravine. I dreamt of England, dreamt so vividly that when I awoke the vision had left a longing for the reality. I struggled against it, but—bah!—when a man fights himself what chance has he of victory? I decided to come—I came —I am here."

He strode up to the fire, extending his hands towards the blaze.

"Dear me — dear me," said Sir Fielding, strangely bewildered by the deep voice, the strange gesture and the foreign accent, as much as by the singular manner of the man. "I heard no carriage drive up."

Maurice faced round.

"Nor do I see how you could, considering that I trod your moor and heath from north to south, and fought my way against a greater storm than those which carry an avalanche upon their backs. I walked."

"Walked! God bless me!" said the baronet, "then," catching at the cloak, "you must be, you are, wringing wet. My dear sir, this is enough to give you your death!"

Maurice Durant smiled a smile without a particle of mirth in it."

" Death !" he replied. " Death will not come to me clad in a cold. I have slept in a damper clothes than these, and found them frozen in the morning. Take no heed of me, but rather of your carpet, which I am gradually spoiling."

" Never mind the carpet," said Sir Fielding hastily, and walking towards the bell. " You must change your clothes immediately. I will tell them to see that my own room will be got ready for you ; meanwhile if you will accept my son Chudleigh's, in which you will find a fire ——"

Maurice Durant held up his hand with a gesture almost of impatience.

" Sir Fielding, I shall be gone in five minutes. Cease I beg of you, for it pains me to give you a refusal. A whim seized me to take one look at the hall. I fought my way here through the storm, and standing outside this window, was drawn hither by your daughter's music. Why should I stay? I have seen her whom I left a child ; you, whom in the old time I had more than a friendship for, and there is naught left for me but to return," and with calm composure and a majestic grace, he swung his cloak round him and held out his hand.

Sir Fielding stared at the stern, weather-tanned face with its deep wrinkles and great piercing eyes in astonishment.

"Impossible!" he exclaimed. "You cannot again brave such a night as this, it would be an insult to me! At least," he added, hastily, as Maurice Durant shook his head, "at least you will stay and eat something ?"

Still the stalwart figure held out his hand, and Sir Fielding grew despairing as he saw the heavy forehead darken impatiently.

"Well, if you will neither rest nor eat, at least you will wait and see Chudleigh ?" he cried.

"I think not," was the reply. "I shall get another opportunity soon perchance. At this moment I am anxious to be on my road again."

"Where are you going—where will you sleep?" asked Sir Fielding, in utter bewilderment, and feeling powerless before the stern will which proclaimed itself in such gravely musical tones. "The village, Maurice Durant, is a long way; there is no inn on the road, not a single place that will open its doors to you to-night——"

"Save one," said Maurice Durant, in a significant tone.

"Which?" said Sir Fielding.

"The Rectory," replied the other. "I sleep in my own house to-night."

Sir Fielding shuddered.

"No, no!" he breathed, "you shall stay!" and going to the door he called out:

"Chudleigh!"

Chudleigh came down stairs with a promptititude quickened by curiosity, for he had never heard his father's voice raised so loudly before.

"Chud," commenced Sir Fielding, with agitation, but before he could get farther the traveller stepped forward and, laying his strong hand on the baronet's trembling arm, said in a deep grave voice, quickened by the rich foreign accent :

"Chudleigh Chichester, your father would keep me prisoner in his castle, and I am forcing my way out ; you are a friend to freedom and will sympathise. Sir Fielding, it is not right to break one's oath. I have vowed to sleep beneath no roof in England before my own. Good-night!" and raising his cap with a gesture of farewell he strode to the door, and before either Sir Fielding or his son could recover from the commanding charm of his manner, it had swung to behind him, letting in a blast of icy wind and a shower of sleet.

"Good Heavens!" exclaimed Sir Fielding ;

"how changed. I seem to be dreaming! Maurice Durant! Maurice Durant!"

"Maurice Durant," breathed a low voice at his side, as Maud's trembling fingers clasped his arm. "Oh! was that Maurice Durant?"

CHAPTER VI.

"With voice despairing, grim, and dread,
He hurls his thunders at their head."

IT was Sunday morning. The storm of Friday had cleared the air, and the sun, washed brilliant by the sleet and rain, and blown quite awake by the wind, shone down on Grassmere, and lit up the ice-bound ways and whitened fields, until they reflected his genial beams like burnished silver set with innumerable diamonds.

The little church in the dale was slowly filling, the simple villagers strolling up the clean-kept gravel path in complete families, and clustering round the porch in conversational groups.

It wanted ten minutes to service time, and they were waiting for the gentlefolks to arrive, for these simple folks considered it a part of

their religious duty to form a line for Sir Fielding Chichester and the "people of the Folly,"
as the Gregsons were called, to pass through,
and be courtesied to, and they no more thought
of neglecting it than they would have left un-
done any other of the few duties of their life,
which they had been taught from the cradle up.

Five minutes to eleven, and there came the
rattle of a carriage—Sir Fielding's, followed by
Lady Mildred's—Sir Fielding in his dark, old-
fashioned coat and frill, looking every inch a
Chichester, and Chudleigh with Maud on his
arm, looking as handsome as even the good
people of Grassmere, who were used to good
looks in their lord's family, could desire.

Carlotta, who accompanied Lady Mildred,
excited much unobtrusive curiosity, dressed in
her deep mourning, edged with sable, and
received as respectful a recognition as Lady
Mildred, who, next to Maud, was perhaps the
favourite.

At the porch Maud stopped for a moment to

inquire after one of the labourers' wives who had been ill, and Chudleigh, seizing the opportunity, approached Lady Mildred.

"Well, Chud, we thought you had lost your way the other night or got drowned as you had not come to see us. I don't think Sir Fielding would have been guilty of such unpardonable neglect."

And she shook her head reproachfully.

Chudleigh glanced at Carlotta.

"Had I known that you were so anxious to see me, my dear aunt, I should have ridden or walked over without fail. Have you got settled yet? Do you feel at home?" he said to Carlotta.

"Quite," she said; "one could not be otherwise, the house is so beautiful, and Lady Mildred is so kind."

"I am glad you like the cottage," he said, eagerly. "Did you hear the storm on Friday?"

"Hear it," she said, with great surprise. "It was terrible. We thought the house would have been swept away. The old Rectory must have suffered much, I should think. I felt a positive relief at seeing it still towering above the old trees."

"Ah, the Rectory," said Chud. "By the way, I have quite a piece of romance for you. You remember the history I told you the other morn——"

"Come, Chud," said Sir Fielding, "it is time to get to our pew."

So Chudleigh had to keep the story of Maurice Durant's return to tell at some future time.

Scarcely had they taken their seats than the Folly carriage drove up, glittering with plated harness and magnificent liveries, and Mrs. Gregson, the son, and the two daughters, alighted, accompanied by a tall, military-looking gentleman, dressed in the height of fashion, and with the most extreme care, so striking the villagers by his languid manner, and filling them with admiration of his golden hair and sealskin coat, that they forgot the customary scrape, and stared as if he were some strange animal.

With much rustling of silks and satins, and passing to and fro of dazzling footmen, bearing books and hassocks, the Folly settled down, then the mild-faced curate ascended the plain, oaken desk, and commenced in the weakest voice possible to read the Morning Prayers to his "Dearly beloved brethren."

The Prayers were finished, the Litany droned through, and the Ten Commandments drearily recited, and Sir Fielding was serenely preparing to wake up for the hymn which the choir had been practising the whole of the week, preparatory to setting himself again for the sermon, when a half-audible buzz from the congregation drew his attention to the fact that the little curate, instead of marching off to the vestry to exchange his surplice, had taken his seat in one of the altar chairs, as if he had quite finished his part of the service, and was prepared to rest.

Before Sir Fielding had recovered from his

astonishment at the unusual proceeding on the part of the curate, the vestry door was heard to close, and the next instant a figure of commanding height and bearing, attired in an old black-brown robe of time-worn silk, strode across the chancel, and entered the pulpit.

The whole congregation were too astonished to do aught but stare at the grand head bent over the cushion in the introductory prayer, which rang out in a deep, grave voice, as unlike in its full, rich music the good little curate's piping, as the strains of a cathedral organ are to the squeakings of a church mouse.

Then when the head was raised the villagers and gentlefolks drew a deep breath, and, fixing their eyes upon the calm, set face, stamped with a true nobility, and marked by deep, heavy lines above the large, stern eyes, waited for the text ; all, excepting those who remembered Gerald Durant and his son, wondering who it was that had come down upon them with the air of a Roman emperor and the face of a king.

Sir Fielding drew himself up, and gazed
round with a look of bewilderment, and, turning to Maud, who was still kneeling, her sweet
face turned up towards the pulpit, with an
expression of wondering awe almost piteous,
whispered :

" Maurice Durant."

She did not seem to hear him, but slowly
rising from her knees as the text " All is vanity
and vexation of spirit " rolled through the
church, and clinging to Sir Fielding's arm,
listened to the sermon with her eyes fixed upon
the preacher's face.

What a sermon it was! Commencing in
slow, measured tones, the man who had fought
his way through storm and wind sufficient to
appal the stoutest heart, explained the short,
curt line, " All is vanity "—explained it with
unflinching severity—a severity and harshness
that were terrible in their depth and eloquence,
and then, warming with his subject, poured
forth upon the heads of the spell-bound con-

gregation a declamation and a denunciation so
terrible in its merciless sternness, so bitter in
its despair, so touching in its hopeless remorse,
that when he had finished—his face lit up with
an unyielding austerity that was awful in its
rigid lines, and his strong white hand resting
heavily on the oaken side of the pulpit, as if
weighted with a crime — every soul drew a
breath of relief, and shuddered as they waited
for the Benediction. But they waited in vain,
for with the same gesture he had used in throwing his cloak round him, he turned, and with the
same firm, commanding step, looking neither to
the right nor the left, descended the pulpit
stairs, crossed the chancel and was lost to sight.

Amidst a death-like silence the little curate,
white and frightened, approached the altar rails,
and in faltering accents delivered the Benediction, which Maurice Durant had either forgotten
or purposely omitted.

Then the congregation hurried out to crowd
the porch and path with eager and curious

groups, inquiring who the strange clergyman was, to find their curiosity farther heightened by hearing those who had remembered him declare that the man who had thrilled them to the heart so wondrously was none other than the long-lost Maurice Durant.

Sir Fielding, with a hurried request that Chudleigh would take charge of the ladies and a reminder that Lady Mildred and Carlotta were to dine at the Hall, hastened to the vestry in time to see the curate, still agitated and frightened, remove his surplice, aided by the old clerk, the only person in the room.

"Where is Mr. Durant?" asked Sir Fielding.

"I don't know, sir," replied little Mr. Hawes, piteously. "He was not here when I came in. Dear me, sir, I am so startled I can scarcely compose myself. Did you ever hear such a serm——"

"When did you know Mr. Durant was going to preach?" inquired Sir Fielding, cutting short his bleating.

"Only this morning, sir," was the reply. " I was just putting on my surplice when the door opened, and thinking it was Mr. Price here, sir, I didn't turn round until I heard a voice—such a voice, too!—say, 'Are you the curate?' I turned round, pale and startled I must confess, and said that I was. 'I am Maurice Durant, your rector,' said he. 'I wish to preach here this morning. Have you the key to that cupboard?' and he pointed to the old press where the robes are kept. I told him I had not, and was going to ask him for some proof, some further explanation, but before I could speak he walked to the cupboard, and with a turn of his hand wrenched it open. Then, taking the old silk gown you saw him wear, he said, 'The bell has ceased—go!' and too confused, Sir Fielding, to offer any resistance, I went. Oh, dear, I sincerely hope there is nothing wrong; if so, it is sure to come to the bishop's ears."

"There is nothing wrong, Mr. Hawes," said Sir Fielding. "It is Maurice Durant who

preached this morning. Make your mind
easy, and remember that however strange his
manner may be, he is your rector," and without waiting for the curate's expression of thank-
fulness, he turned back to the carriages which
were waiting for him, passing several groups
of cottagers who were eagerly discussing the
mysterious event.

Entering the Hall carriage, which contained
the ladies only—Chudleigh had sent Lady
Mildred's carriage back to the cottage, and
decided to walk—Sir Fielding, in answer to
the shower of questions poured upon him by
Lady Mildred, gave her an exact description
of the scene at the Hall on the night of
Maurice's return.

"And he faced the storm there that night,"
said Carlotta, with quiet astonishment. "It
seemed to me sufficient to sweep a human
being from the earth."

"It was terrible," murmured Maud, shudder-
ing and nestling against her companion. "Think,

Carlotta! he fought his way to the Rectory and slept there, in that deserted, ghostly place where his father fell dead! Carlotta, I think, I know not why, that he slept in the very room—he looked aged to-day even from two days since, aged and wan as if he had seen some frightful sight or endured some fearful agony," and she shuddered, uttering a low sob that alarmed her beautiful companion.

"Hush, hush, Maud," she said. "He has terrified you."

"No, no," exclaimed Maud, eagerly; "he does not frighten me. I feel for him, I—oh, Carlotta, think of his face: it is so kingly, so sorrowful, so sad; I am sure he has suffered, suffered terribly, and I pity him so," and she laid her face amongst the furs on Carlotta's breast.

"Poor Maud," exclaimed Sir Fielding. "It has quite upset her. Into the drawing-room where she was playing alone he found the way unseen by any of the servants, how or by what means I cannot understand, and appeared before her, with the rain streaming from a large cloak which he wore in a foreign fashion, and his hair blown about his head like a figure from a Raphael cartoon.   He startled me so that I am not surprised at Maud being unnerved."

"Of course not.   I confess that I never felt so terrified in my life as I 'did this morning. It was quite terrible,," said Lady Mildred.   "I never heard such fearful eloquence."

"One could only learn in suffering such wondrous knowledge of human passion as he displayed," said Carlotta, in a low voice.

"You are right, my dear Miss Lawley, you are right," said Sir Fielding.   "Heaven knows what Maurice Durant has gone through during his wanderings."

"If his history be half as mysterious as his appearance would lead one to imagine it," said Lady Mildred, "it is a sad one, Fielding."

"Ay, ay," echoed Sir Fielding, sighing.

"Is he at the Rectory still, Sir Fielding?" asked Carlotta, as the carriage drew up at the Hall.

"Yes, I believe so," said he. "I sent Wilson over this morning with an invitation to dine here. I put it in the most supplicating language I could, but I do not know—ah, here is Wilson," he broke off as his valet approached the carriage. "Well, Wilson, have you been to the Rectory," he asked.

"Yes, Sir Fielding," replied the man.

"And did you find Mr. Durant?"

"Yes, sir; I knocked several times, and, receiving no answer, was going away, especially as all the windows were as dark and the place looked as desolate as usual, but as soon as I got down the steps, I saw a tall gentleman sitting on one of the broken terraces, smoking a foreign-looking pipe, and watching me quite cool and unconcerned. "Why are you knocking," he said. I lifted my hat respectfully, for I guessed it was Mr. Durant, Sir Fielding, and

said I had a letter for Mr. Durant. He held
out his hand without a word, and after reading
the letter, fell to smoking his pipe again, as if
he had quite forgotten me. I stood silent some
time, and determined to remind him by a
cough. He looked up with a start, and, thrusting your letter into his pocket, said, as he
walked toward the house, ' Tell your master
that I beg to be excused."

Sir Fielding sighed.

" Strange, marvellously strange. It is like
him. I fancy I can see him at this moment
wålking away, and hear his foreign accent,
which is the most singular I ever heard."

Maud sighed deeply.

" Papa," she said, "what will he get to
eat? Will he have any dinner?" she asked,
anxiously.

" I'm afraid not, my dear," said Sir
Fielding.

" It will not be the first time Maurice Durant
has gone dinnerless," thought Carlotta, for she

had been used to faces that bore the hall-mark of hunger.

And if she was not mistaken she could read a story of want and privation in Maurice Durant's.

CHAPTER VII.

"There are strange creatures with manners queer,
Who crop up in our world from year to year :
Yet of them all—ah, find me, if you can,
A more offensive being than the self-made man."

LYRICS OF SOCIETY.

THE "Folly" was new, so was everything in it, from the lord and master thereof to the gaudy dinner service — carved, stamped, and engraved with the Gregson crest wherever there was room to put it—and the glittering armour ranged down the hall, worn by Mr. Gregson's ancestors, who existed in any age Mr. Gregson's imagination might select.

Mr. Gregson's manners were new too, and striking. A little, short, thick-set man, with a red face, rough head of hair, and stubby iron-gray whiskers, large, lobster-hued hands, which he had a habit of banging on tables or chairs in support of an argument, or to emphasise a command, he looked from head to foot that most obnoxious of individuals — a self-made man, who never can forget his manufacturer.

Of Mrs. Gregson little need be said. She was a worthy woman, who really merited better things than a life made miserable by being placed in a false position.

The son, Tom Gregson, bore a strong resemblance to his father, though his manners were slightly better, and he looked something of a gentleman, though, unfortunately, somewhat of the fast school. Tom Gregson was particular about his clothes, took an interest in race-meetings and handicaps, and never omitted to back his opinion, however trivial the subject upon which he offered it ; indeed, nearly all his sentences commenced or ended with " I bet you two to one," or " I'll take six to four," and the like phrases, which shocked his would-be refined sisters, and made his father use bad language.

Of the girls it would be scarcely fair to speak too critically. They were as well-mannered and unaffected as could be expected of them in such bad-mannered and affected surroundings, were tolerably good-looking, rather showy than beautiful, and extremely desirous of entering the charmed circle of aristocracy, and especially of the Hall, which stood at its head.

Occasionally Tom Gregson made the acquaintance of some smaller stars of the fashionable hemisphere, and, obeying his father's order, would invite them down to the Folly, but seldom succeeded in getting acceptations, for there was no shooting and very little fishing to be had on the Folly grounds, and, as for the hunting, the Grassmere pack was not celebrated enough to tempt a hunting-man of these hard-riding, long-run days.

Sometimes, however, Tom succeeded in hooking a fish, and this Christmas was one of them, for a certain Honourable Clarence Hartfield, having nothing else to do, and feeling rather bored with his own "high-toned lot," as he termed Lord Crownbrilliants and the ladies of his family, had accepted Tom's invitation, and was dangling his patent leather-clad heels, and twirling his golden-hued moustache, in the Folly drawing-room, rather enjoying in a quiet way the persistent toadyism of Papa Gregson, and the outspoken idolatry of the Misses Lavinia and Bella.

Coming home from church with the strange sermon ringing in their ears, the Misses Gregson had, of course, burst into a torrent of chatter, in which, as usual, the Honourable Clarence Hartfield did not join, being averse to hard-talking as well as to all other hard work, and preferring to lie back amongst the soft cushions and listen with half-closed eyes. Besides which Mr. Hartfield had another reason for silence. He was thinking—and that was a great under-taking for one of Clarence Hartfield's class—thinking, not of the strange sermon or the preacher, but of a certain lovely face he had seen in the little church, and wondering where he had seen it before.

So engrossed was he on this especial occasion that he was quite dumb to the volley of excited questions, as to whether he had ever seen such an extraordinary-looking man, or heard such a singular sermon! which the mamma and daughters fired at him, and when the gaudy equipage pulled up with a clash at the door, he lounged off to his room, and was seen no more till dinner-time, when he entered the drawing-room in exquisitely-fitting evening suit, with diamond studs at his white wrists and flashing in his spotless shirt front.

"Oh, Mr. Hartfield, we thought you had gone to bed," said Miss Bella, sweeping up her silken skirts to make room for him.

"Did you?" drawled the honourable swell, in a languid monotone. "I did think of it, but—oh, ah, yes," dropping his eyeglass, and recovering from the fit of abstraction which had seized him before he had laboured through his sentence. "Oh, weally, I don't know why I didn't. Pwaps I smelt something you'd got for dinner that I thought I liked," and he laughed spasmodically.

"A plain dinner, sir, a plain joint and vegetables, sir!" shouted old Gregson, from the fire, before which he was roasting his coat tails, and adding a deeper tint to his crimson hands. "'None of your foreign kickshaws for me on Sunday, Mrs. Gregson,' says I. 'Whatever you may do on other days, let's have wholesome victuals on Sunday.'"

"Oh, papa," remonstrated the girls, while Mrs. Gregson smiled with vacant uneasiness.

But Mr. Gregson was not to be put down. Removing one hand from its cooking, he flourished it and continued :

"I hate the French muck I'm obliged to eat here six days a week. What with your soups with names no sensible man can pronounce, and your made dishes which nobody but an idiot would eat, I'm almost poisoned—almost

poisoned," and the eminent Manchester mer-
chant emphasised the last assertion by turning
round and poking the fire with sufficient force
to knock the back of a new enamelled grate
out, adding to the languid Clarence, "and I'm
surprised a sensible man like you, sir, can eat
them."

"Ye—s, it is surpwising," said Mr. Hartfield,
with deep gravity; "I agwee with you." A
chorus of "Oh, Mr. Hartfield!" "Oh, I do
weally. You don't know how fond I am of beef
and mutton!"

Wherepon, just as Miss Bella had declared
that she doated on mutton likewise, Mr. Tom
entered, and proceeded at once to join the hunt
with:

"Hullo! I'll bet you what you like we've got
beef for dinner."

"What the devil do you mean, sir?" roared
old Gregson. "Isn't beef good enough for you?
Do you mean to turn up your nose at wholesome food, sir?"

"Easy, governor," retorted Tom, thrusting his hands in his pockets and falling into a chair; "who said I didn't like beef? It's good enough, I dare say, when there isn't anything better to be got. Well, girls, what's the text?"

"Why didn't you go and hear it for yourself, sir?" growled the father, ignoring the fact of his own absence. "When I was your age——"

"You were a mighty clever fellow," muttered the dutiful son.

"I thought nothing of walking ten miles to church, twice a day too, wet or dry."

"What an appetite you must have had!" said Mr. Hartfield, chuckling.

"I had, sir. I enjoyed my meals then, and they did me good," asserted Mr. Gregson, "and sometimes I had only a lump of cheese——"

"Papa," exclaimed Miss Lavinia, jumping up to stop those reminiscences of the honest past they were so anxious to bury, "there is the dinner-gong."

So they went in to the plain joint and *et ceteras*, Mr. Gregson snarling on the way at a footman who happened to run against him with some vegetables.

"Mamma, did you see that the Chichesters had a stranger with them this morning?" said Miss Lavinia.

"Do you mean the young lady dressed in black, my dear?" asked Mrs. Gregson.

"Yes. Poor thing!" replied Miss Lavinia. "Black did not become her, did it?"

"No," drawled the Honourable Clarence; "but don't you think she became her black?"

The girls laughed, but not very heartily.

"Really you are so humorous," murmured Miss Bella, adding aloud, "Do you know who she was, mamma?"

"No, my dear," said Mrs. Gregson; "she was in Lady Mildred's carriage. Lady Mildred arrived from Paris only a few weeks ago. She brought this young lady with her, I think."

"By Jove!" exclaimed Mr. Hartfield, "I've got it."

"Got what, sir?" growled Mr. Gregson. "Not a bone down your throat, I hope?"

"No, not a bone," replied Clarence Hartfield, relapsing into his lethargic state; "but—a—the clue to a pwoblem I've been endeavouring to solve all the morning. Given, a young lady's face in church, which you wecognise: quewy, when did you see it?" and he chuckled.

"Have you seen her before then?" asked Bella and Lavinia, eagerly, with an almost painful curiosity.

"Yes," replied Hartfield; "on the Calais boat."

"You came over with them?" suggested Miss Bella.

"Yes," said Hartfield. "It was such fun. Evewybody was ill excepting me," and he chuckled. "Captain said I was a bwick, which, though rather impertinent, was twue;

for a fellow that can come over in one of those wetched boats without being queer must be a bwick."

"And the lady was ill ?" said Bella, feeling some little consolation in the thought.

"No, she wasn't," replied Hartfield. "Not wegularly ill, you know ; only squeamish—ugly word, squeamish, Mr. Gwegson—eh ?"

"I don't see anything the matter with it," was the surly reply.

"Of course you did the polite—eh, Hartfield ?" remarked Mr. Tom, looking up from his plate for the first time. "I'll bet any money you made yourself uncommonly agreeable," and he winked knowingly, bringing down upon himself a suppressed growl from his father, a withering frown from the girls, an "Oh, Tom !" from his mother, and a steady stare through the Honourable Clarence's eyeglass, under which he was beaten back to his plate again.

"How singular ?" said Miss Bella, "quite a coincidence, I declare. How funny it will be to meet as strangers after going through that terrible voyage together."

" We shan't meet as stwangers," said Clarence, quietly. " My people know Lady Mildwed— at least I think they do, and I shall give her a call to-morrow."

Both the girls tried to smile as they said " Yes," but it was hard work, for the demons of fear and jealousy were at work within their bosoms.

Were they going to have their prey taken from their nets at the very moment they flattered themselves they were hauling him up?

Dinner went rather slowly after this, an offer of Mr. Tom to bet four to one that Flurry colt would win the county handicap bringing down an outbreak of his father's volcanic language, which ran through the remainder of the course, driving the aristocrat into the smoking room, and the ladies to their place of refuge, the drawing room, where they sat in solemn conclave, discussing with much anxiety and dis-

quietude the projected visit of their guest to
Lady Mildred, and searching their poor brains
to find some means of preventing it, for they
read in the Honourable Mr. Hartfield's sudden
fit of abstraction the symptoms of a sudden
fancy which boded no good to their hopes.

But all their little plots and plans, consisting
of seductive offers of a skating trip, and a long
walk on the morrow, could not induce Mr.
Clarence Hartfield to give up his intended visit,
and on the following morning they had the
mortification of seeing him, dressed with even
more than his usual care, start on his way to the
Cottage.

*   *   *   *   *

"The Honourable Clarence Hartfield," said
Lady Mildred, reading the card which a servant
brought her. "Why, Carlotta, my dear, that
must be the good-looking gentleman who was
so attentive on board the packet. I am sure
that was the name I heard."

"How strange," said Carlotta. "Do you know him, Lady Mildred?"

"That is just what I was asking myself," said Lady Mildred. "Hartfield, Hartfield! Dear me—yes, I remember. I know his people, my dear. All right, James," and in a few minutes the Honourable Mr. Clarence Hartfield entered.

The usual salutations were gone through, and Mr. Hartfield, quite at home in a lounge chair, was calling to her ladyship's mind several little parties at which they had met, when Lady Mildred, with her usual suddenness, said :

"Mr. Hartfield you are quite ignoring the subject, but I must insist upon thanking you for your kindness during that frightful journey. I do not know what we should have done without you. It was strange I should not have remembered you."

"Not at all," said Mr. Hartfield, who was conversing with a great deal more life and much less langour than he displayed at the

Folly, "not at all. I don't think I showed more than the tip of my nose, which is not a very wecognizable feature—eh, Miss Lawley? Besides, it was so dark, and there was so much confusion, that in fact I never expected you to wemember."

And Mr. Clarence smiled with due humility; then, turning to Carlotta, said:

"The voyage must have twied you severely; nasty twip. By Jove! I've heard fellows say that they'd sooner go to Pewu than to Pawis by water. They couldn't go by any other way, though, could they?"

Carlotta smiled; the question did not admit of a verbal reply.

"I am staying at the Folly," he continued. "Do you know the Gwegsons?"

"I had never seen Grassmere before we arrived three weeks since," she said.

"Charming ladies the Misses Gwegson are," said he. "Do you know them, Lady Mildwed?"

Her ladyship shook her head, and smiled blandly.

"We have not met," she said, significantly.

Mr. Hartfield, not a bit nonplussed, drawled on.

"That's a pity. Your ladyship would find them intewesting girls—vewy amusing, by Jove! So is Mr. Gwegson, most owiginal,"—and he smiled—"quite a chawacter in his way, you know."

"Yes," said her ladyship, and, anxious to change the subject, she asked after the condition of the ice.

"First wate," replied the exquisite. "Do you skate?" he inquired of Carlotta.

"A little," she said. "I am very fond of it."

"Why didn't you say so, my dear?" said Lady Mildred. "We could have gone to the pond."

Carlotta smiled.

"I never thought of it," she said. "Besides, I had no skates."

Clarence Hartfield looked up eagerly.

"I'll tell you better fun than skating," he said, "that's sledging. Its glowious, Lady Mildwed! I had a sledge coming down from London, it ought to have been here a week ago, but the wascal forgot to send it. Will you permit me to bwing it over some day and give you and Miss Lawley a ride."

"You are very kind," said Lady Mildred, looking over at Carlotta, across whose brow a cloud swept swiftly. "You would enjoy it, my dear, would you not?"

"Very much indeed," replied the beautiful girl, with a smile. "It would be delightful!"

"Delightful! I'll bwing it!" exclaimed the aristocrat, with a chuckle, rising to go. "I'll bwing it, and we'll dwive all wound the lake— eh? Ha, ha!"

He laughed with quiet enjoyment, in which Lady Mildred, immensely amused at his languid delight, joined, and Carlotta, though the cloud swept once across her brow, chimed in.

Before the concert had drawn to a close, the door opened, and Chudleigh was announced.

He started with a slight frown—though why he should frown he knew not—at the sight of the honourable swell, but bowed courteously as his aunt made the two men known to each other.

A few words passed between them on the usual topic, the weather, and then Mr. Hartfield made his adieux, muttering as he lounged towards the Folly :

"Deuced nice girl. By Jove! wonder if she is the old lady's niece—no welation whatever should say from the likeness; how absurd! I mean the no likeness. And that long, big bweasted fellow is Sir Chichester's son. Looked rather annoyed at seeing me there. Wonder if he's sweet on that girl. By Jove! she's a queen. Clarence, my boy, you're hit, you're hit, Clarence!"

Meanwhile Chudleigh was trying to recover his temper and make himself agreeable.

"Maud asked me to bring you this," he said, handing a small parcel to Carlotta — "some piece of spider spinning, as I call crochet, or wool-work," he added, smiling.

"No," she said, cutting the string. "It's a volume containing some engraving I want to copy," holding it out to him.

"You draw," he said, "or paint?"

"Both a little," she replied. "I am very fond of the pastime, and waste a deal of good paper and colour over my fancy."

"Nonsense, Carlotta," said Lady Mildred. "Chudleigh, get her to show you her sketch-book," she added. "I am going to see the gardener, who is waiting."

Chudleigh looked supplicatingly.

"Will you show it me?" he said.

"Yes," she said, "if you would really like to see it," and going to a bureau she took from a drawer a small portfolio. "There they are," she said. "I am ashamed to let you see them, they are such imperfect daubs."

"Daubs!" he exclaimed, reverently taking one up, and starting with something like pain, for in the beautiful sketch before him he saw the evidence of an accomplishment which added an increased lustre to the beautiful girl, who seemed already in beauty and talent far above his reach. "They are wonderful," he said, quietly. "I'm no artist myself, but I feel assured that these are beautiful. Will you let me show them to Sir Fielding?"

"No, no," she said, hastily, in her eagerness laying one white hand upon the portfolio.

Chudleigh looked surprised. There was something more than deprecating modesty in the frightened tone and gesture.

She noticed his look of surprise, and her face paled.

"Excuse my refusal," she said. "They would give no pleasure to Sir Fielding; they are worthless, believe me. You see, I may safely say so, although you have been kind enough to praise them, because you own that you are no artist, and, however unsuccessfully, I have been a student of art."

All this she said hurriedly, and as if with the object of covering the pained " No, no," with which she had refused, but Chudleigh's curiosity, backed though it was with the reverence a growing love inspires, was too deep to be evaded.

" Why were you so alarmed at the idea of my father seeing them ? " he said, with a smile.

She looked at him for a moment with a strange expression in her eyes.

" If you must know," she said, " I will tell you, Mr. Chichester. These sketches are painful mementoes of a bitter, very bitter past, when I painted them and their fellows for my daily bread. Can you guess why I should not like the records of my poverty to display themselves in the luxury of Chichester Hall ? "

Chudleigh dropped the sketches and turned towards her, his face as pale as hers and his lips quivering.

"Can you forgive me?" he murmured, brokenly.

At the sight of his face and the sound of his distressed voice, her own self-possession, which she had never lost for a moment, became strengthened, and, laughing lightly, she said, holding out her hand:

"Forgive you! What for, Mr. Chichester? Rather let me ask your pardon for a piece of silly sensitiveness."

He took her hand, and, pressing it within his own strong one, was about to raise it to his lips, when the white fingers were calmly but resolutely withdrawn, and the next moment Lady Mildred's entrance put an end to a scene which was not altogether a painful one for either Chudleigh or Carlotta.

CHAPTER VIII.

"Oh, Love was once a little boy,
 And oftentimes a fool;
Yet they who'd gain experience
 Must learn it in his school."

FILLED with curiosity though they were, the inhabitants of Grassmere had to restrain it in the direction of the rectory, for nothing could be more mysterious, silent, or unsatisfactory than the conduct of its owner.

Since his appearance in the church he had been seen but twice—once when he had traversed the village in search of an old woman who had .been hopelessly dumb for years, and to whom he consigned the care of the Rectory —and again when he visited the carpenter with instructions to replace the broken wicket with a strong oaken gate and the glassless window panes with blackened wood.

With the exception of these repairs, if repairs they could be called, the Rectory underwent no other renovation for its master.

Two rooms were cleansed from their time-honoured dust, some of the old oaken furniture with its faded velvet and armorial bearings were carried into them, and in these Maurice Durant lived, buried from the world.

Since his curt refusal of the first invitation, Sir Fielding had deemed it best for awhile to leave the strange being undisturbed, although every one at the Hall and the Cottage was most anxious to see more of him, and, with the exception of Maud, continually talked of him.

She, singularly enough, kept closed lips whenever the subject was brought up, and listened sometimes with a pained flush to some remark of Chudleigh's concerning Maurice Durant and his strange retirement.

Indeed Maud had undergone some change since that evening when the tall figure had startled her by its sudden appearance, and had grown quiet and somewhat pensive, sitting thoughtfully alone where she used to be singing blithely, and often relapsing into a fit of abstraction during the meals at which she was wont to be the light and colour.

Sir Fielding was perhaps too engrossed with his beloved books and the ever-present cloud of the foreclosing mortgage to notice the change, but Chudleigh had seen it and troubled over it, but had deemed it best to let it pass uncommented on, thinking, perhaps, that her melancholy and depression were but the effects of the strange scene on the night of Maurice Durant's arrival.

On the Sunday following that on which Maurice Durant had preached the little church was crammed, all expecting that they should again see and listen to him, but at the end of the Communion Service the little curate mounted the old pulpit, and the congregation was doomed to disappointment.

Maud, who as the service had progressed had drawn closer to Sir Fielding, drew a breath of relief not unmingled with pain when she saw that the rector would not preach, and Sir Fielding, looking down upon her face as she knelt devoutly through the valedictory prayer, saw it flush and pale by turns.

On Wednesday the Honourable Clarence Hartfield provided the gossips with new material for conversation by driving through the village at break-neck pace in a gaily painted sledge, the tinkling of whose bells as they shook on the harness brought Lady Mildred and Carlotta to the drawing-room window of the Cottage.

"Dear me, there is Mr. Hartfield and the sledge," exclaimed Lady Mildred. "What a beautiful little thing it is. I had no idea he really meant to bring it, had you, my dear."

"Oh, yes," said Carlotta; "he looked like it.

Hush, here he comes," she added, as the door opened and admitted Clarence Hartfield, enveloped in sealskin.

"Haw! here I am, you see. What do you think of the sledge? I told the wascal who made it it was too highly coloured, but he said, 'Oh, no; can't have sledge too highly coloured,' eh! eh!"

"It is very pretty, I am sure," said Carlotta. "Is it quite safe?" she added, smiling.

"Safe!" exclaimed Mr. Hartfield. "Safe! I could dwive it full of eggs. Besides, the horse is the quietest thing I ever knew. Ay, you could dwive him if you liked—would you like?"

Carlotta smiled.

"I should not mind, if there were any occasion for it," she said.

Clarence Hartfield laughed.

"She's vewy quiet, but she won't stand in the cold long," he said.

Accepting the intimation, the ladies left the room to don their furs.

It was certainly very delightful gliding over the ice-bound roads and flying across the lake on the very wings of the wind, and Carlotta's face grew very red and her eyes bright, in the clear, crisp air, while her lips were wreathed in oft-repeated smiles at the fervour of her companion, whose *blasé* manner was gradually giving way each moment to a stuttering delight that made every " r " a " w," and filled the air with his Dundeary laugh.

On their way home they met Chudleigh and Maud, who were going in the direction of the Rectory.

Lady Mildred asked Clarence Hartfield to pull up, which he did just in front of the grave face of Chudleigh and the slightly pale one of Maud.

" We have had such a delightful ride, Chud," said her ladyship, " thanks to Mr. Hartfield. Isn't this is a singular vehicle ? "

" Very," said Chudleigh, glancing at the gaudily painted affair. " Quite Continental. I

congratulate Mr. Hartfield on the acquisition
of such a curiosity, and implore him to tell
me whence he procured it."

Carlotta looked up gravely at his slightly
sarcastic tone, and their eyes met. She lowered
hers immediately, while her cheeks flushed with
the slightest *soupçon* of crimson, and he looked
away with a sharp spasm of jealousy. She
looked so bright and happy—was it only the
fresh air and exercise, or the congenial companionship of the Honourable Clarence? he
asked himself.

"Where did I get it?" replied Clarence.
"'Pon my word I don't think I shall let the
secret out; everybody will be having a sledge,"
and he laughed, murmuring to himself: "That
fellah's quizzing me, by Jove!"

"You need not be under any great appre-
hension on that score, Mr. Hartfield!" said
Chudleigh, laughing at the piece of simple
conceit. "Our frosts are not usually severe
enough to warrant the building of such a piece

of magnificence as this," and he laid his hand upon the carriage.

Meanwhile Maud was answering a question of Carlotta's.

"When am I coming to the Cottage, dear? Oh, as soon as Chudleigh will bring me."

"What's that, Maud?" said Lady Mildred. "Waiting for Chud? We'll soon bring him to book. Chud," turning to him, where he stood, patting the horse's neck, "come over and dine with us to-morrow, and bring Maud. Perhaps I can prevail upon Mr. Hartfield to join us!" and she flashed round upon Mr. Clarence.

"Most happy, I'm sure," said he, with evident pleasure, while Chudleigh stood hesitating.

"Thanks, aunt; we shall be very glad, shall we not, Maud? Seven, as usual, I suppose?"

"Yes, seven," said Lady Mildred. "Now, girls, you must bring your conference to an end."

And the next minute the sledge was on its way again.

"Who is Mr. Hartfield, Chud?" said Maud, as they walked briskly on.

"I don't know," said Chud, absently. "A son of the Earl of Crownbrilliants, I think. He's staying at the Folly."

"Staying at the Folly, and driving Aunt Mildred and Carlotta," laughed Maud. "Where are his manners?"

"Perished, with his sense, at his birth," said Chudleigh, curtly, adding, more graciously, "Not much of ill-manners about it; Lady Mildred knows the earl and countess, and the Folly is Liberty Hall, I believe, to all its visitors; though I expect the Misses Gregson are not over-pleased at the defection of this curled fop—"

"Curled fop, Chud!" laughed Maud. "How severe! I am sure he is very good-looking—"

"Very pretty, indeed, said Chudleigh, "I

have seen nothing to equal him since I poked
the eyes out of that wax doll you had when
you were a child ; but "—and he laughed rather
bitterly—" he is a fascinating fellow, no doubt
—at least to judge from the happy faces of
Lady Mildred and Miss Lawley."

Maud looked up quickly and read poor
Chud's secret in a minute, but, with a woman's
wisdom, took care not to let him know what
she had learnt.

" I don't think Carlotta was overjoyed," she
said. " She is scarcely the girl to be much
flattered or delighted at the attention of such
an exquisite as Mr. Hartfield seems, although
he is as pretty as my poor doll."

" Did you think she looked bored, eh ? " said
Chud, eagerly.

" Quite as much bored as amused," said
Maud, pouring balm over her brother's wounds.
" I am glad we are going to-morrow, Chud.
I was afraid we should not see Carlotta for
some time."

K

"I was over there yesterday," said Chudleigh, trying to look indifferent.

"Were you?" said Maud. "You didn't tell me, you naughty boy."

"Did I not?" said Chudleigh. "I was only just passing, and——What's the matter?" he broke off to inquire, as he felt Maud start, and looking down saw her staring in front of her amongst the trees.

"Look!" she said breathlessly. "What is that?"

Chud looked, and saw the tall form of Maurice Durant leaning against the trunk of an old oak, his head bent upon his breast, one hand grasping a fowling-piece, the other hanging white and shapely by his side.

The long cloak had been discarded for a short coat made of wolves' fur, which, fitting tightly, displayed the magnificent figure to the best advantage. The Corsican cap was still retained, but at the present moment it was lying at the feet of a huge mastiff, who, hearing footsteps, raised his head, and with an ominous growl sprang at a clear bound over the ruined hedge and stood ready to spring at Chudleigh.

At the sound of the dog's growl its master looked up, and, striding forward, uttered a command in some foreign tongue, at the same time springing over the hedge and advancing to where Chudleigh, pressing Maud to his side, stood with stick upraised on the defensive.

At the sound of its master's voice, however, the dog dropped on the ground with instant and most perfect submission, and Chudleigh, turning round with a whispered "All right, don't seem frightened" to Maud, said :

"Good morning ; that is a fine dog of yours, Mr. Durant."

Maurice Durant raised his dusky eyebrows.

"That is gracious of you, Mr. Chudleigh Chichester, considering that my rough beast has somewhat frightened you. He is harmless," he continued, crossing to Maud, with a perceptible softening of his deep voice—" harmless as a child where he is told to respect. See !" and raising his hand he spoke again in some foreign tongue, and the dog, with a whine of humility, commenced dragging itself on its body towards Maud.

"You could slay it as it lies now," he said, "and it would not resist. Have you recovered from your alarm sufficiently to stroke it ?"

Maud looked up, and meeting the commanding gaze of the dark eyes, felt bound to obey, so stretching out her hand she touched the dog's head.

Immediately the animal, with a joyful snort, commenced licking her hand, and, with all a girl's love for a big dog, Maud bent down and put her arm round its shaggy neck, murmuring coaxing words, which seemed to fill the dog with delight, Maurice Durant and Chudleigh looking down at the beautiful pair in silence.

"You are friends now?" said Maurice Durant, so suddenly that Maud started.

"Quite," she said, in a low voice, lifting her large eyes timidly to the weather-beaten face above her. "He is a beautiful dog. Will you tell me his name?"

"His name is Tigris—not because he is like a tiger, but because he has fought one and killed it. Hast thou not, Tigris?"

At the sound of its master's voice the animal bounded to his side, but at a gesture from Maurice returned to Maud, who had now gained an upright position, and stretched itself at her feet again.

"Do you find much sport?" said Chudléigh, glancing at the gun.

Maurice Durant shrugged his shoulders.

"No," he said, "not much. I fear I have scarcely sought it with sufficient earnestness. My gun accompanies me as a companion as much as anything else. It is an old favourite."

Chudleigh looked at the weapon of foreign

make, with its barrel covered with strange devices.

"There are plenty of birds in the Hall chase," he said. "Will you not honour us by thinning them? Sir Fielding took it for granted that you would consider the grounds as well as the Hall at your disposal."

"Sir Fielding Chichester is most kind, but the Rectory grounds afford me sufficient scope for what little shooting I require," he added courteously, but with sufficient coldness to bring a hurt expression upon Chudleigh's face.

"I am afraid we shall never be able to induce you to quit your solitary life, Mr. Durant," he said, with a grave smile. "I am commissioned by my father to entreat you to dine with us to-day, but I fear there is little hope of prevailing upon you to accept such a *sans ceremonie* invitation."

Maurice Durant's face clouded for a moment, and his piercing eyes wandered first from Chudleigh then to Maud, where she still knelt at a little distance beside the dog.

Then he said, slowly, and with a sad, grave smile, that gave a mournful charm to his words :

"Mr. Chichester, you are right in thinking I love my solitary life, and am loth to leave it, even for a day. I have lived by myself without a friend—save the dog there—in city and in waste—alone ! Solitude has become almost a necessity to me. I am unfitted for the social life. Still, to prove to you I am not quite the hermit and anchorite I see you half think me, I will dine with you to-night."

"You will?" said Chudleigh. "Sir Fielding will be delighted; for myself——" He stopped, for his eager manner had brought a regretful reluctance upon the dark face, and he feared that the promise would be withdrawn if he continued.

"We dine at seven," he said; "but if that is too early, or a later hour than your usual——"

"My usual hour for dinner," said Maurice

Durant, "is when I need it. Seven, eight, or any time will suit me equally well."

"Then we shall expect you at seven," said Chudleigh.

"I will be with you," replied Maurice Durant, and with a slight inclination he turned away.

Maud looked up, and saw him walking quickly from them, and, patting the dog, joined Chudleigh, who was standing looking after the strange being whom he remembered as the open, light-hearted boy of twenty.

"Mr. Durant has consented to dine with us to-night, Maud," he said, as his sister came up and took his arm.

Maud started and looked up with a sudden flush, but said nothing, and walked on.

"Hullo!" said Chudleigh, with an exclamation, upon coming up to where Maud had left the dog, for it lay there motionless, with its head turned in their direction and whining, "here's the dog," and he attempted to send it after its departing master. But the dog refused to move, wagging its tail and fawning upon Maud. "What a nuisance," said Chudleigh. "I must run after Durant and tell him. It will never do to leave the animal here," and he leaped the broken hedge and walked quickly in pursuit of Maurice Durant, calling the dog, who still, however, stuck fast to his post beside the beautiful girl.

Maurice Durant looked round as Chudleigh, touching him on the arm, said :

" Will you call your dog ? He seems to have taken a fancy to my sister, and does not look inclined to follow you."

" Your pardon ! " he said, raising his eyebrows, " I had forgotten the dog."

He turned and walked quickly back to the road, saying to Maud :

" I told Tigris to stay by you, and he would do so unless I recalled him until the day of his death."

Maud looked up with surprise.

"And leave you?" she said, with an innocent artlessness that was charming.

"Ay," replied Maurice. "Tigris knows that the best part of affection is obedience."

"And he would have followed me home?" said Maud, looking wistfully at the dog, who was stretched at her feet.

"Yes, and shall do so if you wish it," said its owner, reading the wistful look with a calm smile. "He is yours."

"No, no," said Maud, eagerly, even pushing the dog's head away with her tiny hand; "I would not deprive you of him. He is the only——" "being you have to love," she was going to say ingenuously, but stopped and flushed painfully.

"The only thing I have to amuse me," he said, intentionally misunderstanding her sudden silence, and adding, with a smile, "Not so; there are still the trees and the rooks and my gun. Tigris shall go with you, and if you tire of him, why he can join his master's broken fortunes again," and lifting his cap from his head he left them once more, this time un-followed.

Maud stood looking after him with a pale face and wonder-filled eyes.

Chudleigh regarded her for a moment in silence, then with a laugh said:

"Come, Maud, and bring your prize with you. By Jove! never was anything presented with a more royal air. He is like a prince in an old-fashioned romance, and the dog is as noble."

"Not so noble as its master," said Maud, in a low voice. And Chudleigh, looking down at her lowered face, saw, with some surprise, that her eyes were filled with tears.

However, he merely whistled, and they walked on, the dog trotting calmly by Maud's side, as if it had never owned another master.

CHAPTER IX.

" Nor may we e'er forget
    The follies we commit ;
Fate reaps in after years
    Full harvest of our tears."

DINNER was over, and the drawing-room at
the Hall was shining softly in the light of
the tall wax candles, which burnt with a
delicious softness that our modern aching eyes,
accustomed to the garish glare of hideous gas
chandeliers, know nothing of.

Sitting in a velvet chair, the dark blue of
which made her fair skin look whiter and
purer than ever, Maud, gazing at the fire with
dreamy eyes, was thinking of the scene that
had occurred in the morning, and, with Tigris's
head resting on her tiny foot, was weaving

an imaginary history of the man who was
sitting beside her father and brother in the
dining-room ; for Maurice Durant had kept
his promise, and arrived at the Hall at half-
past six.

When Maud entered the drawing-room before
dinner she started, the tall form, attired in
an evening suit, with its grand face, from which
the long, thick hair was brushed in a mass
of rugged curls, leaving the forehead bare
and white, looking strangely handsome, was
so great a contrast to its wild, almost savage,
appearance of the morning.

Still, though clad in the uniform which so
seldom becomes an English gentleman, Maud
felt a strange pleasure in the consciousness
that Maurice Durant looked not one whit less
noble in the black coat of fashion than in
his tunic of wolfskin.

One thing that struck her at once was, that
whereas her father and Chudleigh both wore
a few articles of jewellery, Maurice Durant's

only trinket was an antique ring, with a dull,
leaden-looking stone set in it.

Maurice Durant wore neither watch-chain
nor ornamented studs, his shirt, down the front
of which ran an edging of foreign work, being
fastened with black stones, which were cer- .
tainly not ornamental, whatever their intrinsic
worth.

· At dinner he had eaten little, and drank
scarcely more than a glass of claret, and, save
for a few remarks addressed to Sir Fielding,
had maintained a thoughtful, somewhat abstracted, silence. Still, his manner and, more
than all, the grand cast of his face, kept his
taciturnity from offence, for it was impossible
to measure Maurice Durant with the rule
applied to the ordinary run of men ; and,
indeed, Sir Fielding was too pleased with the
success of his attempt to coax his strange
neighbour to the Hall to risk losing him for
ever by forcing him into unwilling conversation,
trusting that in time the strange reserve would

melt before the constant warmth of unobtrusive friendship.

Besides which, Sir Fielding had not forgotten amongst his books sufficient of his knowledge of the world to be long in surmising that his guest had undergone sorrow and trial enough to warrant the strangeness of his manner and speech. So that the dinner had gone off very quietly, Chudleigh and Sir Fielding carrying on a rambling conversation, Maurice Durant breaking in suddenly with a question or remark, always to the purpose, and Maud speaking seldom, and listening when Maurice spoke with a rapt attention.

After she had withdrawn to the drawing-room, Sir Fielding rang the bell for a particular old port, but Maurice Durant declined any more wine.

" If you will not taste my old port," said Sir Fielding, smiling, "you will have some more claret and a cigar."

But these also were declined, and, after a

glass with Chudleigh, Sir Fielding led the way into the drawing-room.

Tigris rose as his master entered, and sprang towards him ; but, holding up his hand, Maurice Durant spoke two words in the same language in which he had bidden him follow Maud, and the dog returned instantly to its place.

"That's Corsican, is it not?" said Sir Fielding, who had caught the words.

"Yes," said Maurice Durant. "Do you speak it?"

Sir Fielding shook his head.

"No, unfortunately," he said ; "but I chanced to know the two words you spoke. Is the dog Corsican?"

"Yes," said Maurice, almost curtly, and, turning to a picture, changed the subject by saying, after a few minutes' examination : "A Carlo Dolci?"

"Yes," said Sir Fielding. "It is good, is it not?"

"Very," was the reply. "It is the finest

head I have seen of his save one that hung above an altar in a small Florentine chapel.''

"There are several good pictures in the gallery," said Chudleigh. "Would you like to see them?"

"Much," said Maurice Durant, "if it would not be giving you trouble. I am fond of pictures."

"And music?" added Sir Fielding, interrogatively.

"And music," assented Maurice Durant, his face lighting up suddenly. "Had we more music the world would be a brighter one."

"And a better," said Chudleigh, ringing the bell as he spoke.

"Is there a fire in the gallery?" asked Sir Fielding of the footman who appeared.

"Yes, sir," said the man. "Mr. Chichester's instructions were that it should be lit during the frost."

"Ah, yes; I had forgotten," said Chudleigh. "Shall we go there? Come, Maud."

L

The three made their way through the hall and up the spacious oaken staircase to the long gallery lined with various pictures and the family portraits.

For some minutes Maurice Durant examined the pictures in silence, moving slowly on. But coming upon the grand organ, which stood in a recess built in the middle of the gallery, he exclaimed, with an unmistakable air of pleasure :

" An organ ! "

" Yes," said Chudleigh. " I must crave your forgiveness for not mentioning it before. I ought to have known you would like to see it."

Maurice Durant bowed slightly.

" It is a grand one. I know the maker."

" Will you try it ? " said Sir Fielding. " I fear it has lost some tone, for Maud seldom touches it, and I never."

" Do you not like the organ ? " asked Maurice, turning suddenly to Maud.

She started at the abruptness of the question, and hesitated as she replied, faintly:

"Yes, but I cannot play it well enough, and it—it seems almost wrong to trifle with its grand music."

Maurice Durant looked at the pale face with a sudden interest.

"Will you play for me?" he said, gently, fixing his dark eyes upon hers.

She would have given worlds to be able to refuse, but she could not, for the request, soft-toned as it was, sounded like a command.

Trembling in every limb, and flushing for an instant, she sat down to the instrument and played a "Gloria," her quivering fingers almost refusing to press the keys.

Maurice Durant's face grew thoughtful as the music swelled out, and when she had finished he inclined his head gravely with courteous thanks.

"Your objection to the instrument would soon lose its colour did you but play oftener," he said.

"If I were sure——" she hesitated, flushing at his mild praise.

"You may be," he said, laying his hand upon the carved oak of the organ. "Give it more of your love and it will give you more of its music."

"I will play more," she said, in a low voice; then, hesitating, she said:

"Will you play?"

His eyes looked a negative for a moment, and he shook his head; but suddenly he moved, and instead of turning away seated himself at the organ, playing some subtle piece of music quite unknown to Sir Fielding, who was no poor musician in theory, and the like of which for sweetness and sorrowful grandeur the listeners had never even imagined.

First there floated through the vaulted gallery a low, solemn wail, which might have been the ghosts of the departed Chichesters chaunting in unison a song of the spirit world.

Mournful to a degree, it brought the tears to

Maud's eyes, and caused Sir Fielding's head to droop upon his breast. Gradually it swelled out into a burst of grand harmony, that rang echoing and re-echoing like the joyful acclamation of a choral multitude, then suddenly changed to a soft, delicious melody born of a dream, and so, gradually growing lower and more mournful, died away like the sighing of a summer breeze.

For a second there was a dead silence, the steady, subdued light falling upon the magnificent head of the player as it bent over the instrument, and upon the beautiful one of the young girl, also bent—but to hide her tears. Then Sir Fielding rose from the seat he had dropped noiselessly into, and advanced towards the organ.

Maurice Durant started at the sound of his footsteps and rose, turning his face, upon which rested such an expression of perfect serenity and peace as might have befitted a saint, but seemed marvellously strange upon those sorrow-marred features.

"Thank you, thank you," said Sir Fielding, in a low voice. "I never imagined anything so beautiful."

"Nor I," said Chudleigh, coming from behind, his face likewise moved. "Surely, Mr. Durant, you must be the most glorious organist that ever lived!"

The musician shrugged his shoulders, his face having lost the softness, and grown as stern and impassive as ever.

"You have only to visit any Italian cathedral to hear better playing than poor mine," he said. "Your organ is a fine one; it should never be silent a day."

"It never should be if I had my choice," said Sir Fielding, eagerly, "and you should be its interpreter, Mr. Durant. It is waste of words to assure you that the greatest service you can do me is to use the Hall, and everything pertaining to it, with the utmost freedom. Beside the organ, I am afraid we have nothing to tempt you in the slightest; but if that does, let me entreat of you not to resist it."

Maurice Durant bowed his head.

"Your hospitality is Arabian, Sir Fielding," he said. "But, as regards the organ, let me remind you that you have one who can interpret it nearer home," and he turned with a slight smile to Maud, who was standing with her hands clasped, gazing thoughtfully at the keys, her ears drinking in eagerly the tones of Maurice Durant's voice.

She looked up with earnest eyes, in which the teardrops still glistened, and, shaking her head, said :

"I shall never touch it again. It would be desecration."

He shook his head.

"You make me regret my little theme," he said. "If you will retract your declaration, and will permit me, I will send you the score for it."

She looked up with a flush of pleasure.

"If you will send it me I will try to play it," she said, earnestly.

"Good," he said, smiling. "It is a contract. I will write it for you to-night."

"Ah," said Sir Fielding, catching at the admission, "then it is your own composition."

But there came no reply, and Sir Fielding, regretting his hasty speech, recalled attention to the pictures. But canvas, glowing as it might be, was but poor fare after the rich repast they had enjoyed, and, although Maurice Durant seemed willing to examine the masterpieces closely, Sir Fielding was anxious to take him into the library and Chudleigh to get him to the piano.

Maud had sunk into a seat and let them go on without her. She could still see them and hear every word spoken however.

"That is a fine piece of colouring," said Maurice Durant, looking at a dark Dutch landscape. "You have a fine collection, Sir Fielding," he added, "the older ones especially."

"The more modern ones are in the smaller corridor leading to the library," said Sir Fielding, eagerly. "There are some there you would recognise, I have no doubt. Shall we go?—that is if you are not wearied."

And he led the way down a smaller oaken staircase than the one by which they had ascended.

"This is the nearest way to the smaller gallery," said Sir Fielding. "It——" He broke off suddenly to turn round with astonishment, which soon changed to alarm as he saw Maurice Durant, who had not yet commenced descending, leaning against the heavy balustrade in an attitude of terror or some other strong emotion, his face livid as death, even to the lips, and his eyes, which were fixed on a small painting of a woman's head, all ablaze with light.

Chudleigh turned at the same moment, and, uttering an exclamation of alarm, hurried to Maurice Durant's side.

At the same moment Maud sprang from the recess.

"Papa, papa," she cried, in agony. "He is ill, he is dying!"

And as if forgetful of everything but the distorted face, she flung herself on her knees, and seized Durant's hand, which hung rigid and lifeless at his side.

At the sound of her voice, and still more at the touch of her trembling hand, the stricken man lowered his eyes from the staring, mocking ones of the picture, and with seemingly a tremendous effort overcome the thralls which bound him.

Standing upright, and pressing his closed hand against his heart, he turned with a smile upon his curved lips to the terrified Sir Fielding, who exclaimed :

"Good God! What is the matter? Are you ill, Maurice?" using in the excitement of the moment, the simple name that had once been so familiar.

"A mere trifle," was the reply, in hoarse yet regular tones. "I am unfit for polite society, Sir Fielding; I frighten it. A mere nothing," he continued, holding up his hand with a gesture almost of command as Sir Fielding was about to speak. "A sudden pain at the heart with which I am on intimate terms. I beg you not to distress yourself farther concerning it; it is the veriest trifle, the merest puff of wind——"

And, for the first time since they had seen him, he laughed a low laugh of strange, subtle music, that thrilled through them somewhat as the wailing of the organ had done.

"And now for the smaller corridor," he said, abruptly. "You have piqued my curiosity, Sir Fielding, and I am anxious to satisfy it."

And he turned aside without glancing even in the direction either of the small picture before which he had succumbed, or at the beautiful girl who had flown to his side, and who stood at a little distance gazing on his face with a reverent solicitude.　Perhaps the avoidance on both sides was intentional.

*　　*　　*　　*　　*　　*

It was midnight.　The Hall was dark, its guest had departed for his own house—the dreary Rectory—which looked more ghostly than ever with its one solitary, dimly-lighted window, behind which paced to and fro the strange owner.

The broad brow was more marked, the thin lips, sterner and more unbending, and the eyes fiercer yet sadder than ever, as, never pausing in his monotonous striding up and down the chamber, with its faded old-world furniture and worn tapestry, its rows of dust-covered, carved book shelves and rust-eaten armour, he muttered :

"To the ends of the earth, even here, she follows me!　Oh, God! how dire is thy vengeance!　Here, where I had flown for solitude and refuge—here, where I had meant to dwell apart from all—here, within the shadow of the

noble house I have brought to ruin and desolation—I find her gibing, mocking, fiendish
face."

Here the bitter soliloquy broke off, while
the speaker hid his burning eyes in his clenched
hands and groaned.

But presently the voice, which rose and fell
with a low, tremulous sound, like the cry of
a being in mortal agony, caught up the thread
of thought and spun it into words again, the
communer unconsciously using the sweet-toned
" thou " and " thy " which had become familiar
to him by his long sojourn in foreign lands.

" Whither wilt thou go, Maurice Durant?
Whither wilt thou go to forget thyself and
the dreaded past? In the frozen seas thou
wouldst see her face reflected on the ice ; in
the desert thou wouldst see it traced in the
sand! Fly! of what avail is flight? Thou
canst not fly from thine own black heart!
Thou canst not escape from thine own memory!
No, no, a thousand times no, no. The past

bears bitter fruit — deadly wine which thou must drink to the dregs. And yet how hard! oh, God, how hard! How different might have been thy lot! Thou idiot, thou idiot! didst thou never dream of some fair face like that of the sweet, pale lily that caressed thy world-worn hands to-night? If thou hadst, thy dream would have saved thee!"

Then came another pause, but the voice, this time slower, softer, yet with more of pain in its determination, breathed forth:

"Thou must go, Maurice, before the ill is done; the sweet face is creeping into thy heart, and the sweet girl-eyes already bear within them the dawning of love. Love! oh, bitter mockery that so pure a being should love thee, Maurice Durant. She must not, she shall not," he continued, throwing up his hands and gasping as if for breath. "Save her, Maurice; fly and save her if thou wouldst not merit the hell which awaits thee!"

CHAPTER X.

" Cursed be the forms that err from Nature's golden rule !
Cursed be the gold that gilds the straitened forehead of
the fool ! "

" I LOOK upon dinner, Miss Lawley, as one of the most important things in life," said the Honourable Mr. Hartfield, shaking his curled head with profound earnestness, and crossing his long legs with an air of comfortable ease. " You look as if you thought me wrong. I'm right, I assure you. I know a fellow—he's vewy old—said he'd tried everything—by Jove ! fighting, travelling, working, marrying—but all turned out blanks, nothing a prize except his dinner. He's a—a—what's his name ?— Solomon—you know, eh ? "

The scene was the drawing room at Lady

Mildred's. Dinner had just come to an end. Sir Fielding was comfortably esconced in an easy-chair beside the fire, opposite Lady Mildred, who, with Maud at her side, was recounting some travelling experience.

In a corner of the room, Chudleigh, with an album in his hand, was leaning, watching Carlotta and the Honourable Clarence, who were seated on an ottoman.

Mr. Hartfield's voice, as it rose and fell, floated over to him, jarring upon his ears most discordantly, and set him wondering with a fiery impatience how the beautiful Carlotta could sit and listen with such smiling attention.

"Can you find no higher aim or end than dining, Mr. Hartfield?" said Carlotta, with a slight smile. "What would become of the world if all its inhabitants thought with you?"

"Good! by Jove!" murmured the exquisite. "That's a poser. Not that I care for the world, you know; no fellow does."

"You have not answered my question," said Carlotta.

"I can't," replied Mr. Hartfield; "it's so like a widdle, and I never could make out a widdle. I took a magazine in once—you know what I mean; not a p-powder magazine, but a monthly journal. It was vewy good, you know—all stories and poetry; but there was always a page of c-conundrums and enigmas at the end; and I used to turn to this page —not because I wanted to, you know, but because I couldn't help it. I was f-fascinated, er, er!—difficult word, fascinated—and—— Where was I? Oh, the widdles. Well, they used to stick in my mind for days and months, and I always used to be asking my-self and sometimes other fellows why a p-pastrycook is like St. Paul's Cathedral, and all that sort of thing!" and, overcome by the ridiculousness of the idea, the honourable gen-tleman leaned back and burst into a ripple of "eh, ehs!" in which Sir Fielding and Lady

M

Mildred joined, for it was impossible to refrain from laughing at the absurd tone and manner of the fashionable exotic.

Chudleigh dropped the album with suddenness enough to make them all jump, and crossed over to the fire, and Maud, looking up, saw the frown upon his face, and, pitying him, rose from her seat and crossing over to Carlotta, said :

" Will you sing something ? "

" Ah do, my dear," said Lady Mildred ; and Carlotta rose and walked towards the piano, which Chudleigh opened for her, saying, in a low voice as he did so :

" It was a shame to disturb you."

She raised her eyes for one moment to his cloudy face, and seemed about to answer him, but dropped them again without speaking, and commenced playing.

Chudleigh leaned against the piano with his arms folded across his breast and his head lowered thoughtfully.

Mr. Hartfield had exchanged his seat for one

beside Sir Fielding's chair, and at the pause of the song Chudleigh heard his father say, in answer to some question of the exquisite's :

"Mr. Gregson and I don't meet very often. I regret to say that I am not of much use in parochial affairs."

"You ought to know him, weally," said Mr. Hartfield. "He's a vewy good fellow—wough, you know, vewy wough, but made of the wight sort of metal."

Sir Fielding bowed.

"I am glad to hear you say so," he said, mildly.

"Oh, yes, he is, I assure you," said Mr. Hartfield, who, for some reason or other, seemed bent upon championing his friends. "Here's an example—I don't like examples, they remind one of arithmetic as a wule—one of your bulls got into his flower garden the other morning and did no end of d-damage. Now another fellow would have p-pounded the animal and made a disturbance—eh ? But Gwegson didn't,

by Jove! He went about by himself vocifera-
ting for a quarter of an hour, and then had the
bull driven back into your m-meadow, and set
his man to mend the hedge. That's owiginal—
eh? By Jove!"

"It's more than original," said Sir Fielding,
warmly. "It's generous and gentlemanly. I
will lose no time in writing to thank Mr. Gregson."

"By Jove! you mustn't do it that way, you
know," said Mr. Hartfield, quickly, shaking his
head. "Gwegson would know I'd split on him,
and—by Jove! Oh, I say, you know—eh?"

"I understand you," said Sir Fielding, smiling
at the enigmatical objection. "At least, I must
thank him in some way."

"May I suggest that you wide over to the
Folly to-morrow morning?" said Mr. Hartfield.
"I'm sure you'd like them. They must be
good-natured sort of people to let a fellow go on
his own hook as I do. Twy them, as the twades-
people say, Sir Fielding. It would weally be a

kindness—eh, Miss Chichester?" and he turned
to Maud with a smile.

"Do call, papa," said Maud. "It was very
good of Mr. Gregson, was it not?" and, leaning
over, she touched Chudleigh—who, as he was
bending over Carlotta and saying something in
a quiet, eager voice, started at the interruption—
and told him the incident of the bull and the
flower-garden, adding, in a lower tone: "See,
Chud, papa has almost given way. Do persuade him to call."

Chudleigh nodded acquiescingly, but not with
any show of pleasure, and, seating himself beside
Carlotta, continued the conversation, if conversation it could be called when he alone was
speaking, Carlotta listening with lowered face
and eyes.

"The horse is quite safe. You know I would
not let you ride it if it were not. Say you will
come. Give me your promise. Maud will be
so delighted ; she is fond of a gallop, you know.
Let me bring the horse round for you to-

morrow morning if the weather be bright, will you?" and he waited eagerly for the answer, which she seemed loth to give. "I know you are fond of riding," he continued, persuadingly, "for I heard you tell Maud that you were, and I am sure you will like 'The Sultan.' You will come, will you not?"

With a troubled look and a slight flush she raised her head and almost said yes, when the Honourable Hartfield came lounging up to them, and, with a start, Carlotta regained her usual calmness, and said:

"No, thank you very much; not to-morrow, please," and Chudleigh, giving a stern frown at the exquisite as he passed, rose and walked up to Lady Mildred.

"Aunt," he said, "I have a few letters to write to-night. You will excuse me, will you not?"

"Not going yet, Chudleigh?" said Lady Mildred. "Dear me, how is that? The carriage will not be here for another hour, will it, Sir Fielding?"

"No," said Sir Fielding, looking up at Chudleigh. "Must you go, Chud?"

"Yes, sir," he replied, and, shaking hands with Lady Mildred, he went to the ottoman.

"Good night, Mr. Hartfield," he said, as cordially as he could, and "Good night, Miss Lawley," as icily.

Poor fellow! It was an unhappy time for him. It seemed hard that such an idiot as the Honourable Clarence appeared to be could win smiles from the woman he loved, whereas he gained nothing but cold looks and cold words.

CHAPTER XI.

"Here comes the aristocrat
With courtly mien and gait;
While close upon his heels
The men of money wait."

BE the Honourable Mr. Hartfield's reason for bringing about an acquaintance between the Hall and the Folly what it might, he certainly had arranged his tactics in an astonishingly masterly way and successfully, for the morning after the dinner at the Cottage, Sir Fielding and Chudleigh rode over to the large red-bricked house which they had so long ignored.

Hartfield had advised the Gregsons of the intended visit in a few languid, offhand words, and the family were on the *qui vive* of expectation, old Gregson being warned in a timid way by his daughters to keep watch and guard over his language, and Tom counselled to absent himself altogether during the interview, or to keep a prudent silence, and on no account to offer to " lay " Sir Fielding two to one, or bet him the odds.

Notwithstanding these preparations, the Gregson family were extremely agitated when Sir Fielding and Chudleigh dismounted and were ushered into the drawing-room.

" How do you do, Sir Fielding," said Mr. Gregson, grasping the long white hand in his short red one. " Happy to see you. Quite an honour, sir. Hope you're well, Mr. Chichester. Mrs. Gregson : my daughters, Misses Bella and Lavinia. Met Miss Maud at the Mothers' Meeting, I believe, several times."

Sir Fielding and Chudleigh then passed over to the ladies, who, all smiles and flutterings, made room for them on the sofa, old Gregson seating himself in an easy chair and commencing a conversation—concerning the weather, of course—with Chudleigh.

Sir Fielding, between the two girls, was highly amused for some few minutes, not insensible to their evident attempts at blandishment, and, thinking after all that they were rather well behaved and quiet, said :

"My daughter would have accompanied us this morning, but she has a headache. I am commissioned with her compliments, which I beg of you to accept. Will you do us the honour of calling at the Hall when next you are near ?"

Mr. Gregson bowed, and the girls murmured "Delighted." Then Sir Fielding rose and commenced the real object of his visit.

"Mr. Gregson," he said, "I owe you some thanks. Permit me to discharge the debt."

"What's that, sir ?" asked Mr. Gregson, bristling up from his chair. "Wasn't aware of any debt. No thanks due to me for anything that I know of. Don't quite understand, Sir Fielding."

"You have added to your generosity by forgetting it so quickly," replied Sir Fielding, with his quiet, courtly smile. "I have come to apologise for my bull, and express my regret for the damage and annoyance which his tresspass must have caused you. I only learnt it yesterday, or, be assured, would have found an earlier opportunity to thank you for your consideration."

"Nonsense, nonsense!" retorted Mr. Gregson, slowly relapsing into his old manner at the warmth of Sir Fielding's apology. "Bulls will be bulls. He didn't do much harm, and if he had I suppose that wouldn't be any reason why one gentleman should forget himself in regard to another. I'm about sure if one o' my cattle had got on to your grounds you would have acted something after the same style."

Sir Fielding coloured slightly, for he had a shrewd suspicion that Mr. Gregson's bull, had it trespassed on the Chichester grounds, would

have gone into the pound ; therefore he thought
it safest to bow.

"Just so," exclaimed Mr. Gregson. "'Do
as you'd be done by' is my motto, and always
has been since I first started in life. I commenced on that principle and went along on
that principle, and I'm going on it now," and
he brought his heavy fist down upon a *papier
maché* table with sufficient force to make Sir
Fielding jump and Chudleigh smile.

"A very good principle," said Sir Fielding,
his soft, well-bred voice presenting a marked
contrast to the burly one just silent. "With
such a principle a man should prosper."

"And I have prospered, Sir Fielding," replied
Mr. Gregson, looking round with a defiant air.
"I have prospered. I began life with two and
fourpence halfpenny in my pocket, and here I
am with—well, it doesn't matter how much.
I'm content. I've worked hard but uprightly.
This hand may be hard but it's honest," and
Mr. Gregson flourished his right hand before

him with a decided shake of the head, while
Sir Fielding muttered beneath his breath :

" It is hard."

" I've worked my own way, sir, I may say
unhelped, unaided. I've known what hardship
is and the bitter crust, and I've known what
misfortune is; but hardship and misfortune
don't hurt a man; it's luxury and ignorance,
extravagance and vice, as ruins a man, and
that's what England is coming to."

Mr. Gregson having delivered his opinion,
emphasised by another bang on the unoffend-
ing table, sat down.

Sir Fielding smiled.

" Your life must have been an interesting
one," said he.

Then, turning to the window, and anxious to
change or rather avoid a continuance of the
subject, he said :

" That is a fine position for your fruit
trees."

" Yes, very good," said Chudleigh. " Miss

Gregson tells me that their gardener got the prize at the last show."

"Three prizes," said Miss Lavinia, modestly.

"Dear me!" said Sir Fielding, who within his heart had cherished the idea that no plums could compare with the Chichester.

"Would you like to walk round?" said Mr. Gregson, and, Sir Fielding assenting, the three gentleman made their way into the conservatories.

Sir Fielding was astounded at their magnitude and appointments.

"This is very beautiful," he said, with admiration.

"That arrangement for the firs is a splendid improvement," said Chudleigh. "Maud's ferns would be improved if she adopted this plan."

Mr. Gregson looked pleased.

"Well," he said, "they are nice, I suppose. They ought to be, for they cost a mint of money—a mint of money," and he shook his head slowly. "But, there, I don't mind, it's a whim of my daughters, and they never have a wish ungratified. 'Papa,' they say, 'I want a conservatory. I want a new pony. I want a set of brilliants.' They have them. Conservatory, ponies, brilliants—no matter what they ask for they get it."

Sir Fielding murmured something which sounded like "Indulgent father, value of money," and the three descended the steps on to the lawn.

As they did so, Mr. Hartfield appeared coming round the corner, exquisitely dressed in a loose morning coat of purple velvet, perfectly fitting pearly-gray trousers and a deer-stalker that set off his golden hair to perfection.

Arranging his eyeglass, Mr. Hartfield lounged forward, and with a noiseless laugh of delight shook hands.

"Ah, Sir Fielding, delightful morning, is it not? Ah, Mr. Chichester, can you play racket? Yes! Give me a game, eh? 'em! Points? Oh, deuced bad player, I assure you. Mr.

Gregson, Tom, I mean, beats me frightfully. Ah, by Jove! here is Mr. Gregson," he added, as Tom Gregson, in a brown cut-away coat, light trousers, and horsey-looking deerstalker, emerged from the racket-hall.

"Mr. Chichester, Mr. Gregson. If you want any information about the next handicap, Mr. Chichester, Mr. Gregson's the man. He knows a horse when he sees it. No, no, I don't mean that. I should have said that he's a most excellent judge of horses. Eh, Tom, eh?"

Mr. Thomas Gregson looked half surly, half complimented.

"I am not a bad judge of a horse," he admitted.

"Coming to have a game, Mr. Chichester? Fine game. I will bet you what you like there is not a healthier sport except hunting going. Now, Hartfield, what points?"

Chudleigh shook his head.

"I am very sorry," he said, "I must return with Sir Fielding."

Sir Fielding and Mr. Gregson had gone on to the stables.

The three younger men followed them, Clarence Hartfield talking all the time, and managing imperceptibly to cover Mr. Tom's occasional remarks with his frequent, " Eh, eh ? " and striving, so it seemed to Chudleigh, who, being jealous of the exquisite, was naturally suspiciously keen-eyed, to pass the meeting over pleasantly.

" Hullo, here's the governor," said Tom, entering the first stable. " Look here, Mr. Chichester. I can show you a good bit of horseflesh. What do you think of that ?" and, with a knowing look, he pulled the cloth off a showy-looking animal. " That's a good one to look at, eh ? How do you do, sir ?" he added, turning to Sir Fielding, who at that moment entered.

Sir Fielding shook hands with him and stood to look at the horse.

" A splendid creature," said Chudleigh, with

N

honest admiration. "Rather a tough one, is it not? Its ears look suspicious."

"Tough!" repeated Mr. Tom; "I should guess she is too. I'll bet there is not a nastier-tempered animal in the country. Have a spin round?"

And he jerked his head at the courtyard.

Chudleigh was a good horseman, and did not know what fear was, but it struck him that it would be scarcely wise to get a broken head or a damaged nose simply to contribute to Mr. Tom Gregson's amusement, so he declined.

"Quite right, sir, you're quite right," said Mr. Gregson, senior. "Tom's an idiot with horses, a perfect idiot. This animal, sir, is a beast. Knew it the moment I saw it, but my son insisted upon purchasing it, and consequently there is a hundred guineas gone in a kicking machine," and he waved his hand in denunciation at the obnoxious quadruped, who by its fidgeting to and fro, seemed to understand the lavish condemnation passed ᵤpon her.

"Oh, she ain't so bad as all that," said Mr. Tom. "Look here. Bob says he can't mount her; says she kicks him off as soon as he's on. Now I say 'it's his fault. What does he let her kick him off for when once he's on? Look here, Hartfield; I'll bet you two to one in guineas I mount her and keep her as still as a statue without a kick to the bad."

Mr. Gregson opened his mouth, pretty widely too, but Clarence Hartfield's voice stopped the abuse, or whatever was coming, by drawling:

"Done, by Jove! and tweble if you like."

"I'll double it," said Tom, without hesitation, and telling one of the grooms to come and saddle her.

It was hard work for the man, but after a great deal of backing, kicking, hoisting, and other gymnastics the saddle was slipped on and all ready.

Chudleigh and Sir Fielding looked on with some little astonishment.

To mount the horse alone would be a matter of no little danger, and they had not given Mr. Tom Gregson credit for courage.

"All ready, sir," said the groom, touching his cap.

"Then take her out into the yard."

"Yard, sir?" muttered the groom, interrogatively, "not the paddock?"

"Yard, yard, I said," replied Tom.

"Beg pardon, sir," said the groom, with whom Mr. Tom, through similarity of tastes, was a favourite. "I was thinking of the stones."

"Then you shouldn't think of the stones," retorted Tom. "Go and do as you're told."

The man led the horse out. The animal was as quiet as a lamb, but with her ears laid well back, and her eyes leering viciously.

"Don't you think you'd better try the paddock, Mr. Gregson?" said Sir Fielding, mildly. "A fall on those stones would be dangerous."

"But I'm not going to fall, sir," said Tom. "Besides, the bet was for the yard, and I'll stick to it."

"Don't be a fool," growled his father.

But to this mild exhortation Mr. Tom made no reply, and, followed by the others, walked into the yard.

The moment he approached the horse it reared on its hind legs, then coming down with an ominous crash, struck out behind.

"I'm off the bet if you like, Tom," said Mr. Hartfield. "You'll break your neck."

"I'll treble it if you like," retorted Tom.

"No, it's wobbing you," said Clarence, shaking his head.

"All right," said Tom.

And taking his whip from the groom, he with a sudden spring, vaulted on to the saddle, and, holding the bridle with a grasp of iron, gave the beast a good slash across its satin skin.

Off she went across the yard like a thunder-bolt, then made a sudden stop and an attempt to raise her heels, but with another slash and a peculiar turn of the hand her rider got her mouth well under, and she stood still.

"Keep a look-out, sir!" cried one of the grooms, as the beast, perfectly astounded, laid back her ears right along her neck.

"Confound you! mind your own business," shouted Tom, irately, and the groom slunk away.

"Now then," cried Tom, "she's to stand three minutes."

And with a lash of the merciless whip again he brought her with a leap into the centre of the yard.

Then, stroking her neck, but in no whit lessening the strain on the bit, he kept her motionless almost as a statue, and, as Chud-leigh cried out the third minute, he leapt to the ground with a grin.

"By Jove!" exclaimed Clarence Hartfield,

assuming, with the aid of his eye-glass, a look of astonishment that was perfectly ridiculous, although he had known well that the feat would be performed. "Tom, you are a w-onder. Here's the m-money; and the twick was worth it, eh, Sir Fielding?"

"Beautifully done," assented Sir Fielding, with genuine admiration, adding to Tom, whom he regarded with very different eyes to those which acknowledged his greeting, "If you would do me the favour to look over the stables at the Hall, Mr. Gregson, I think you would find one or two animals there that would interest you."

"You are very kind," said Tom, candidly. "I should be glad to come. To tell you the truth, I'm fond of horses——"

"Too fond," muttered his father, who, though proud of his son's achievement, could not miss an opportunity of growling at him.

"And I'm glad to make the acquaintance of a strange one now and then," he continued.

"Then come over to the Hall by all means," said Chudleigh. "I have just bought a new hack; perhaps you would be kind enough to give me your opinion of him. Will to-morrow suit you?"

"To-morrow will suit me," said Tom.

And with this the gentlemen returned to the drawing-room, where the ladies were anxiously awaiting them.

"Sir Fielding," said Mrs. Gregson, tremulously, "will you and Mr. Chichester partake of a little luncheon? There is some laid in the dining-room, and——"

"Ah, do, Sir Fielding," broke in Mr. Gregson. "I can give you a glass of dry sherry, the Amontillado, Count Laminte, Milan."

"Deuced good," commented Clarence Hartfield. "Let me wecommend, Sir Fielding."

But neither Sir Fielding nor Chudleigh could be prevailed upon to stay, and after a little more small talk and the accepting of invitations to the Hall, father and son departed.

For half a mile on the homeward journey neither spoke, Sir Fielding seeming lost in thought, and Chudleigh, who never on any occasion interrupted his father's meditative mood, walking by his side in silence.

Suddenly, however, Sir Fielding said :

"Well, Chud, what do you think of them ?"

"All is not brass that glitters," replied Chudleigh, epigrammatically.

"That is true, that is true, Chud," assented Sir Fielding, smiling. "I think there is gold beneath the gilt."

"The father is a self-made man, but he is genuine," said Chudleigh. "And his son—well, he doesn't lack courage."

"No," said Sir Fielding. "I confess to some astonishment at the spirit he showed in mastering that animal. I did not imagine he possessed either the courage or the tact."

"I can't say I like him," said Chudleigh, "but I must say I admire his pluck. I suppose we must make them welcome at the Hall."

"Of course," said Sir Fielding, at once, his hospitality horrified at the thought of any half-measures.

Then there came a silence, again broken by Sir Fielding.

"What do you think of the women, Chud?"

"I haven't thought about them, sir," said Chud. "They are very passable. I like Mrs. Gregson, and pity her. As to the girls, well, three weeks of Maud and a month of Miss Lawley"—here his face flushed—"taken consecutively would do them good, I think."

Sir Fielding sighed.

"It is for Maud's sake principally," he said, "that I have made their acquaintance. My darling has been looking unwell lately, Chud—eh? She is nothing nearly so light-hearted as she used to be. Looks pale and thoughtful,—too thoughtful for bright-eyed Maud. What is it, Chud, what is it?" he asked, anxiously.

"I cannot say," said Chud; "I have noticed

that Maud has become very quiet lately, and that she looks pale and *distrait*, but I don't hold the clue, sir. Perhaps she wants a little society, and the Gregsons may do her good: certainly they will amuse her."

" She has never been the same girl since the night Maurice Durant came back."

" Ah !" said Chudleigh, " Have you heard how he is, sir ?"

Sir Fielding shook his head.

" I sent Wilson," he said, " but although he knocked several times no one came to him. Maurice Durant must have been out in the woods and the old woman may have been in the village. Chudleigh, there is some mystery —I fear a dark one—hanging about Maurice Durant. Heaven knows why, but since his return I have never seen him or heard his name without feeling a chill presentiment of coming ill in connection with him. He makes me tremble, yet I cannot help being drawn towards him, and—ah,—Chud, let us change the subject.

What do you think Mr. Gregson asked me in the stable?"

"Impossible to guess," said Chudleigh.

"He wants me to give him, or rather the village, that piece of ground at the end of the green on which to build a school for the children."

Chudleigh sighed.

"What did you say, sir?" he said, in a low voice.

"I did not tell him that every inch of the ground was mortgaged, Chud; I evaded the request, and let him think me a close-fisted miser. Oh, Chud, Chud, if you could know what I suffered in being obliged to refuse that Manchester cotton-spinner a piece of ground, and for such a purpose, when he himself, mark you, was willing to spend his gold in building the school, you would pity me."

"I do, sir," said Chudleigh, with a pressure of the hand.

Then they walked on for a few moments,

absorbed in their own sad thoughts, but suddenly Chudleigh looked up with a hesitating
air, and Sir Fielding, reading it in a moment,
said :

"What is it, Chud? what are you thinking
of?"

"I do not like to tell you, sir," said Chudleigh.

"Why not?" asked Sir Fielding. "Speak
out, Chud, speak out."

"Well, if you insist upon it, sir," said· Chud,
still hesitating. "An idea has just struck me.
It pains me to refer to the subject, sir, but I
cannot help it."

"You mean the mortgage, Chud?" murmured
Sir Fielding, without raising his head.

Chudleigh nodded.

"There seems no lack of money there, sir.
Mr. Gregson might——"

Sir Fielding winced as if Chudleigh had
struck him an actual blow.

"Don't speak of it, Chud! I'll think it over.

Oh, Chud, Chud, the Hall under the thumb
of a Manchester cotton-spinner!"

*   *   *   *   *   *

Great was the congratulation at the Folly
as to the visit just brought to an end.   Mr.
Gregson's head was up an inch higher, and
his voice, strange to say, a tone lower; perhaps Sir Fielding's soft accents had influenced
it.   Tom Gregson was in a state of radiant
self-satisfaction, and the ladies flushed with
pleasure and delight.

"We have to thank you for this pleasant
morning, have we not?" murmured Miss Bella
in Clarence Hartfield's ear, forgetting her
affectation in her overwhelming joy.

Clarence Hartfield smiled.

"Eh? Told Sir Fielding that you'd get on
well together. I was wight, you see. Always
am, eh? Mr. Chichester jolly fellow, eh?"

"Oh, very nice!" said the girls, warmly.
"So grave and gentlemanly—quite a second
edition of Sir Fielding."

"He! he! Thought you'd like him," said Clarence, rising slowly. "I'm going to have a glass of shewwy. Will anybody come and see I don't drink too much?"

Then, with another noiseless laugh, he lounged into the dining-room, where, behind his glass, he could chuckle unobserved, and mutter:

"What a deuced clever fella' you are, Clawence, my boy! Wegularly netted the whole of 'em! With Miss Bella and Miss Lavinia dancing wound him, he won't have much time to dance wound Miss Lawley—beautiful Carlotta!—and so leave the course clear for you, Clawence, my boy. He! he! this fella' is not half such a f-f-fool as he looks!"

In which latter assertion the reader will perhaps give Mr. Hartfield credit for some truth.

CHAPTER XII.

"By the pricking of my thumbs
Something wicked this way comes."

SHAKSPEARE.

THERE are some parts of Hatton Garden, pretty as its name is, where a well-dressed person could not be reasonably secure of retaining his watch and chain, or indeed his life, if he did not look well after it. There are courts and alleys cutting through its dark, noisome streets that are blind in more senses of the word than one; tall, dark, dirt-stained houses, mysteriously occupied, and guarded as carefully as the Bank of England; and small, disreputable-looking public-houses, behind whose grease-marked doors,—which swing with a noiseless, furtive sort of secrecy peculiar to the atmosphere and surroundings, swarthy faces and queerly clad beings sit plotting and planning, drinking and frowning, playing the eternal dominoes, and occasionally stabbing each other, with a perseverance in the carrying out of foreign manners and customs astounding in this great city of ours.

Wending our way through the close-smelling thoroughfares, bordered on each side by dens of misery and filth, at the doors of which lounge dark-hued Italians with blackened pipes in their mouths, or black-eyed, sallow-looking children sulkily squatting in the gutter or the kerb, let us penetrate an alley—dark and dismal even in the spring sunset—and, pushing open the low door of the heavy-browed public-house which stands at its end, pass into the small sawdusted space before the bar.

Three men are standing there, all of them dark, swarthy-visaged, with jet-black, twinkling eyes, the fire in which smacks of ferocity and the quick flashing of cunning. Thin lipped, high cheek boned, and compact of limb, one would at once judge them Italians.

Silently for a time they lounge moodily against the greasy bar and its partition, occasionally lifting their wine-glasses—for they are drinking pure Rhenish, the like of which could not be obtained at any aristocrat's dinner, imported, stored, and sold only to his own particular customers by the Italian landlord of this dirty public-house—and puffing at the tiny cigarettes which they hold between their white teeth.

At last the eldest one glanced at the clock, stretched himself, and said, in the patois of an Italian village:

"He is late."

"When is he not? Tell me, Piété," retorted the second, flinging himself down upon the hard wooden bench and supporting his head upon his long, sinewy hand.

"Your English is always late!" said the third. "He is all promise, but no perform.

He will swear you to punctuality with an eagerness and solemnity sublime, and keep you waiting half an hour after his own time. Bah! Baptiste, Piété, be patient. You have not endured this abominable clime nor its detestable people so long as I, Jean, have. When you have you will take these things as the English themselves do—quietly," and with a gleam of his white teeth the third lifted his glass to his mouth and drained it.

"Know you aught of this mission, Baptiste?" asked Piété, when the landlord, at a signal from Jean, had filled the glasses and returned to his perusal of an Italian newspaper in a corner of the bar.

"Not a scrap," was the reply. "It is some move of Spazzola's. He told me to wait with you two here till six, and he would come with the instructions; but, by Saint Paulo! it is near seven, and I'm wearied to the death."

"It will not be safe to go," muttered Piété. "What say you—shall we wait, Jean?"

"Why do you ask?" snarled Jean. "You know it is more than our necks are worth to trifle with Spazzola. He tells you, me, to be here—we are here. He does not come—we wait. What else were we to do? what else?"

"Pa! You are ill-grained this even, Fratello Jean. Wine, wine for Jean, that it may soak his humour down."

"St-r-r!" hissed Baptiste, between his teeth. "Cease snarling, wolves—the lion comes!" and he flashed his eyes at the door, which opened at the moment and admitted a tall, fierce-looking Italian, half concealed by a ragged cloak and a sombrero hat, followed by a short, thick-set Englishman, whose flat, bull-dog features, short oily hair, suit of corduroy, and well-worn velveteen, blue spotted neckcloth, and heavy soled boots proclaimed him at once a brother of the fraternity whose unexpected midnight visits at wealthy mansions result in compulsory absence from their native land, for the benefit of their own morals and their country's well-being.

In short, the Italian's companion was a ticket-of-leave man, and looked it as plainly as if he had stitched the ticket on the breast of his jacket.

Raising his eyebrows as a token of recognition, the Italian sauntered up to the bar, and directed a quick gesture at the ticket-of-leave man.

"A go of gin," said he, in a hoarse voice, apparently proceeding from the region of his thick boots. "Hot!" he added, then stood regarding the three Italians with side glances from his small, sharp-set eyes, that were near akin in cunning to their own.

The steaming glass of fiery liquor disposed of at one gulp, and a glass of wine having been finished by the Italian, the latter, nodding to the three others, took the ticket-of-leave man's arm and walked through a low doorway into a dark room, followed by the three others.

The door of this apartment Jean carefully

bolted, then, taking a whistle from his pocket, blew three soft calls.

After two minutes' waiting a portion of the floor at the corner of a room was raised in the shape of a trap-door, and, still without speaking, the five men went down—the trap-door closing after them as noiselessly as it had opened.

At the foot of the ladder by which they had descended was an apartment, something between a cellar and tap-room, the walls unpapered and streaked with the mould of damp, and the floor covered with thick sawdust over which the feet made no noise. Two or three tables, a wooden bench, and a few chairs comprised the furniture of the room, if one omits the broken bottles and glasses and a small tin frame for candles dangling from the roof.

" Now," said Spazzola, dropping into a chair, and motioning to the rest to follow his example ; " now we are safe, let's to business. First, Mon Piété, Baptiste, Jean, let me introduce you to a brother. His name is Bill, his profession is—ours. *Il mio amico*, these are my brothers. Soh! it is good!" he exclaimed, as the man introduced as Bill rose slowly from his chair, expectorated, grasped the hands held out to him, and then sat down again with the air of one who had undergone much in the cause of politeness.

"Baptiste, we will drink."

Baptiste rose, and, touching a spring, summoned a dwarfish, ill-looking ruffian; who came from a side door let into the wood, in the manner of a reptile dropping from the roof, and taking their orders returned in a few minutes with a bottle of wine and enough gin to last several "goes," then, disappearing, left the party free to continue the conversation.

"Any news, Jean?" asked the one called Spazzola, who seemed by his manner and tone to hold the position of head.

"None, Spazzola!" replied Jean. "None, save that money is scarce, wine dear, and our hands idle."

"All which ills I came to dissipate!" retorted
Spazzola. "I have news — perhaps because,
unlike you, I seek it. Hands are idle when
they seek no work, money is scarce when it is
not chased, and wine—bah! wine is always dear
while a rogue keeps the cellar. Soh! I have
news, said I, and good news. Piété, your head,
so long held down like a beat cur's tail, shall
raise itself like a padrone's.

"Jean, your dry throat can, an you choose,
lap Rhenish all the day; and you, oh, slender-
waisted, calf-eyed Baptiste, shall have gold
enough to deck a dozen green-eyed Maries."

And, with a short laugh, he caught up the
glass and emptied it, while the three men,
suddenly roused from their lethargic attitude,
bent forward across the table and fixed their
glittering eyes upon his mocking face.

"It is time," muttered Jean, sinking back into
his chair and lowering his eyes. " Hungry dogs
grow impatient."

"And yelp!" retorted Spazzola. " Enough,

amico. The prelude is over—for the opera.
Piété, you little think of the trouble, the labour,
the travail your Spazzola undergoes to feed you.
You little know the danger. Soh! enough.
For three weeks I have left you to try the
chase. Ay, for three weeks or all but a
day, with no luck, but your waiting horse
wins. Is it not so, *il mio amico?*" he inquired, turning to the Englishman, who nodded
surlily.

"And on the last day, meaning but yesterday
night, I came across my friend here, who was
looking far and wide for Spazzola and his
lambs. That we met was a chance, for I had
dropped into a crowd to try my luck with the
pockets when I saw him relieving a too trustful
idiot of his trinkets. We went to the kitchen
at Whitechapel, stayed the night, and arranged
an undertaking which, by the holy Mary, shall
line our girdles. Listen. There is——Stop ;
let our friend relate himself the plan of the
campaign, for he is generalissimo."

And he slapped the ticket-of-leave man on the shoulder.

Bill got up with a clumsy movement, strangely contrasting with the graceful play of the Italian's limbs, and said, suddenly, stopping to gulp some gin :

"What I got to say won't take half the time you've been palavering in—it's as plain as a pikestaff and as straight as a jemmy. Your mate here came across me cly faken the other evenin' and being ·palish I asked him to go in with a little affair I had on hand. He seemed agreeable if so be I'd take on three more, and, as it's allers in affairs of this kind the more on us the merrier, I agreed."

"And the plot—the affair?" asked Jean, eagerly.

"Is this," replied Bill, looking cautiously round, and lowering his voice till, what with its hoarseness and burglar slang, the three could scarcely follow him. "Down in the country, inland, there's a jolly fine chance of gamey bit

o' cribbing. It's a old house, reg'lar matchbox
stuff to get through, and I believe crammed
full o' swag. The only man as lives in it is
a crazed parson o' some sort; him and a
woman as is deaf and dumb are the only
people livin' in it. There's a dawg, but I'd
manage him. I'm good at dawgs. Next to
the crib itself is a big 'all and several other
'ouses, tidy-sized, so that we could go in for
a hat-full if so be you'd pluck to run it.
Anyhow, this 'ere alone's a good pull and a
safe one, and if you'll stand by a cove, play
fair—mind, no splitting or shirking—we shall
collar a lot o' swag."

Breathlessly the men listened, following each
word with charmed ears and flashing eyes.

" What sort ?" asked Baptiste, in a whisper.

" Plate !" replied the burglar. " Solid lumps,
old-fashioned. I've been told that there's chests
and chests, cupboards and cupboards full of
it."

The Italians rose to their feet with a gesture

of excitement, but Spazzola's raised hand warned them into calmness.

"The cove in the crib is a strong 'un. I've see'd him—went down a purpose. He'd be a tight bit if he turned crusty. There ain't to be no shirking."

A sudden gesture of the Italians interrupted him. They raised their hands, and the steel blades of three stilettoes flashed in the dimness.

"Right you are!" croaked the burglar, hold- out his fist. "Give us your fins."

CHAPTER XIII.

"Yea, Love is lord of all,
Simple and wise;
Strive how we may
He blinds our eyes.
Oh, Lov   our king,
To thee we sing."

ONCE more the Rectory was deserted. When
and how its master had departed only one
person knew, and she—the old housekeeper—
being dumb, could not tell; even if she chose.

Maurice Durant had departed in the night
it was supposed; what direction he had taken
it was impossible to conjecture even, for there
were no traces of his flight, searched for though
they were; for Sir Fielding, even at the risk
of the strange being's displeasure should he
hear of it, had caused careful inquiries to be
made for miles round.

Nothing could be learned.

One man had asserted that, as he lay beneath a hedge on the night Maurice Durant had dined at the Hall, he had seen a tall, dark figure, wrapped in a cloak and followed by a huge mastiff, pass by like a ghost, going in the direction of London, but no further trace could be found, and Sir Fielding, arguing that Maurice Durant must have stopped somewhere for food and drink on the road, came to the conclusion that he had gone farther into the country, or perhaps had, by a circuitous route, reached the sea coast, and so taken ship for the Continent.

That so much mystery should enwrap the movements of Maurice Durant gave him no surprise, for it was impossible to weigh his actions in the same balance with ordinary men.

Much as Sir Fielding regretted his flight, he could not help feeling a certain sense of relief which Chudleigh shared, though why he could not tell.

How much his absence touched Maud it was impossible to say. She never mentioned his name, and her face gave no sign, though the dreamy, wistful, almost indescribable expression that came upon it when Maurice Durant first spoke, never left it.

At the end of two months the Folly and Hall were " hail, fellow, well met."

The Chichester visit had been supplemented by Lady Mildred's, and the Folly had returned them both.

Then invitations to dinner passed to and fro, followed by rides and drives in the fresh spring mornings, and at the Folly a grand ball, at which, owing to Sir Fielding's example, some of the principal county families had appeared.

This overstepping of the high bounds of caste produced good results to both families. It elevated the Gregsons, toned them down, and made them presentable, and brought a fresh dash of interest into the somewhat monotonous life at the Hall.

The Honourable Clarence Hartfield had suddenly been summoned to town to attend the sick bed of Lord Crownbrilliants, so that he was robbed for the present of the fruit of his plotting, but as he had promised to return immediately his father was convalescent, he still rejoiced in the success of his pretty little scheme.

Maud was delighted at the acquisition of new friends, and by her meek, gentle manner, so free from affectation, and so thorough-bred, won the admiring devotion of the Misses Bella and Lavinia directly, to say nothing of her conquest over Tom, which was very amusing.

One morning Tom had ridden over with his sisters to entice Maud into a ride, and, she at once consenting, the four were soon cantering towards the Cottage to call for Carlotta.

A pony carriage dashed round a corner when they had reached the heath, and Miss Bella, who was blessed with long vision, declared that Lady Mildred and Miss Lawley were seated therein.

In another minute her assertion was proved
to be correct, by the pony carriage halting on
the roadway, and Lady Mildred's parasol being
raised to beckon the riding party across.

"Well, girls," said Lady Mildred, as the party
clustered round the dainty little turn-out and
poured forth a stream of salutations. "Mr.
Gregson, how do you do? Carlotta and I are
going to Chudleigh's flower show. How is it
you are not there, Maud?"

"Too early yet, aunt," said Maud; "it was
to take place at three o'clock."

"Two o'clock Chud told us—did he not,
Carlotta?" said Lady Mildred.

"Yes," said Carlotta. "Perhaps he made
a mistake."

"Very unlike Chud if he did," said Lady
Mildred, emphatically. "Are you one of the
judges, Mr. Gregson?"

"No, but my father is, Lady Mildred," said
Tom. "I don't know a cabbage from a ge-
ranium."

"If it were a horse show," said Bella, "Tom would be tolerably competent."

"If it were a bonnet show," retorted Tom, "I know a young lady——"

"Come," said Lady Mildred, laughing. "I won't stay if you're going to teaze each other. As it is, I don't know what to do. If we really are an hour too soon I shall scold Chudleigh."

"Drive round the moor, aunt, and we will gallop round and meet you. That will fill some of the time up," said Maud.

"But you are not going in your habits!" said Lady Mildred, in comic dismay.

"Oh, yes, we are," said Bella. "It is a very unpretentious affair, Lady Mildred. Mr. Chichester allows only the villagers and labourers to exhibit, and the flowers are set out in the school-room. We are to walk through and see you distribute the prizes, and then ride back —isn't that to be it, Miss Chichester?"

"Yes," said Maud. "Chudleigh says it will be so crowded that we must not stay long."

"How thoughtful he is," said Lady Mildred to Carlotta. "Nothing seems to escape him when he is planning anything for the good of the villagers. I'll be bound he will work really hard to-day, give up his luncheon and very likely his dinner, just to please a set of people who really are never grateful."

Carlotta looked down coldly through her veil, which barely hid the sudden colour that tinted her beautiful face.

"I fancy he. does not do it for their gratitude," she said.

"Of course not," said Lady Mildred. "It's a matter of duty with him, and Chudleigh is perfectly Quixotic in his ideas of duty."

Carlotta made no reply, but, turning to Tom, asked him how a certain colt was progressing.

"Oh, very well, Miss Lawley," said Tom. "He'll turn out a good one, I think. He's clean about the legs—pretty head too. You intimated you would come over and look at him, but you have not done so."

"I will," said Carlotta, "believe me."

"I got a letter from Hartfield this morning," said Tom, as Carlotta gathered her reins in hand and raised her whip, the girls having already turned their horses' heads.

"Indeed," she said, calmly, her eyes fixed upon the off pony's head. "I hope Lord Crownbrilliants is better."

"Hartfield says he's the same," said Tom, "but I don't think, from what I hear, that his lordship is likely to pull round."

Carlotta, still keeping her eyes fixed, said:

"I am very sorry to hear that."

"Yes," said Tom, "it's a bad job. Hartfield is the next Lord Crownbrilliants, you know."

The next moment he was alone, the ponies obeying a sudden pull, starting off with sufficient spirit to jerk Lady Mildred's parasol from her hand and spinning away at a pace which Tom mentally pronounced "stunning."

CHAPTER XIV.

" Now, by two-headed Janus,
Nature hath framed strange fellows in her time."—
Shakspeare.

As the sun sank behind the housetops and
the last patch of smoke-dimmed crimson gave
place to the dingy darkness which Londoners
call twilight, a tall Italian walked silently and
with the peculiar stealthiness of a cat down an
old-fashioned street in Chelsea.

Perhaps the rambling wooden houses with
their pointed gables and crossbeams, toned by
time and the gloriously miserable English climate, and spotted here and there by latticed
windows, which seemed to have been designed
for the purpose of keeping out the light as
well as preventing any one from seeing through

them, reminded him of a certain small Italian town in which he had first drawn breath ; or perhaps he was looking for that pretty familiar object, a public-house.

Whatever his purpose he stopped at the middle of the street and, shivering slightly with the cold, although an Englishman would have called the day warm, gazed up and down, muttering :

"Filthy climate! Dante must surely have meant this detestable England when he made his infernal regions of ice. I vow by the saints I freeze on its hottest day. Ugh! What horrid place is this where one finds no wine-shop, no cigar seller? Oh, Spazzola! woe to thee that thou shouldst leave thy Italia for such a purgatory as this befogged and dismal isle! Pah! why do I growl? A hungry dog must take his bone where it is thrown him. Not that my bone has fallen yet. By St. Joseph! I fear me it will never leave the hand of the Fates which hold it. Ha! at last here is a den. Pah! why should I dub myself idiot by

asking for that which they cannot give ? Wine !
They know not what it is. The ambrosial
nectar to them spells p-o-r-t or s-h-e-r-r-y—
thick, hot, sweet, fiery, and altogether detestable.
Ah, Spazzola, thou art doomed to horrid beer,
bitter as gall, heavier than lead, and sour to
the throat."

With this wholesale condemnation of one of
the English leading articles of commerce he
stepped into a low-doored public-house, which,
being within sight of the water, had been dubbed
the "Waterman's Arms," and above its heavy
door bore a fancy portrait of an impossible sailor
rowing an impossible boat on an impossible piece
of water.

This work of art the Italian stopped to gaze
at with wonder and sorrow, and an anathema
on British art, which he transferred to British
beer, as that delicious concoction of malt, treacle,
sugar, blacking, and Heaven knows what besides, rolled down his throat.

Behind the little bar, which was scrupulously

clean, a young girl fluttered about—not serving, because excepting the Italian there was no one to serve.

In her bright blue dress, upon the neck of which fell a shower of black hair, she looked pretty and enticing in the extreme, and Spazzola, a true Italian in his admiration of the beautiful, whether embodied in a graceful waterbutt or a pretty girl, having nothing better to do, sought to forget his disgust for the beer by engaging in a little chit-chat; so commenced by establishing himself in a comfortable attitude, and uttering the remark that there were not many customers.

"No," said the girl, "not in the afternoon. We get them in the evening when the watermen and lightermen come off."

"Come off where?" asked the Italian, with his foreign accent and puzzled raising of the eyebrows.

"The river, of course," replied the girl.

"Ah, soh!" assented the Italian. "And do

not the gentlemen, the—what do you call them?
—the nobles, come and play their dominoes
—eh?"

"Nobles! Bless me, no," said the girl, laugh-ing. There are no noblemen in Chelsea, and
not many gentlemen either. Leastways," she
added, "we don't see them here. In the summer
sometimes the boating gentlemen come down
as far as this, but they're very noisy, and want
serving all at once, and that ain't what I call
gentlemanly. There's no one can pull a pint
of beer quicker than I can, but when it comes
to twenty people wanting twenty pints of ale
and twenty bottles of ginger-pop all in two
minutes and a half I'm not equal to it."

"No. What for do they want 'pop'?"
queried the Italian, to whom, tolerably well
acquainted with the English language though
he was, fresh slang words cropped up daily to
puzzle.

"To drink, of course," retorted the damsel.
"'Pop' is what we call ginger-beer for short."

"Ah, ah! I see, I see," said the Italian, ejaculating in his own language, "Ginger-beer! What will these English not use for their vile liquor? Ginger! Oh, St. Marie! Have you no gentlemen who veesit here of an evening for a little *conversazione?*"

"We don't sell it if they did," said the girl; but gleaning from the puzzled expression of Spazzola's face that she had misunderstood him, caught at his meaning, and added, "Oh, I know. No. Most of the people about here never go out. They're a most unsociable lot. Why, I've knowed some people livin' in this street for four years and only send for supper beer twice the whole time."

"It ees shameful!" said the Italian, looking greatly shocked, though in his heart, considering what supper beer was, he admired them for their abstinence.

"There's another gentleman as has been lodgin' in the street for more than two months, and he ain't been inside the doors, although he always passes after dark."

"After dark!" repeated the Italian, greatly interested in an individual who possessed a habit so particularly his own. "Does he not walk out in the day?"

"No, never," replied the girl, "and when he does go out at night he is wrapped up to such an extent you can't see more than the tip of his nose and his black hair, which, by the way in which it falls about the collar of his cloak, and by the cloak too, which is a beastly thing, just like a foreigner's, I should say as he was an Italian."

"Italian!" repeated Spazzola. "Ees that so? A countryman of mine! I am Italian," he ejaculated, striking his breast. "Where does he live, *la mia figlia?*"

"There, in the top room of that house," she replied, pointing to the top window of an old-fashioned house across the street. "He lives there all day, doing something—working, I

suppose—and comes out like a bat or an owl
at night," and she laughed at the comparison.

"It is strange," said the Italian, his dark eyes
fixed on the ground, thoughtfully. "I think I
will go and speak with my countryman. What
say you, *la mia figlia?* Is he amiable, polite, a
bon camarade?"

"I should say not," said the barmaid. "From
all I have heard I should think he was a regular
crusty old fellow. But why don't you go and
see for yourself? He'd be glad to see a
countryman, if he is an Italian."

"I weel," said the Italian. "I wish you good-
day, senora. The spot is charming, your beer
is superb, and yourself—ah, me! And I once
refused to believe there were angels on the
earth!"

With these last words he stepped through the
doorway, and, looking cautiously round him,
walked slowly up to the house the girl had
pointed out to him.

While he was lounging softly past, meditating

upon the mode in which he should effect an entry, the door opened, and a girl ran across the street to a chandler's shop, leaving the door ajar.

With a mental blessing on the propitious Fates, Spazzola, with the speed and noiselessness of a snake, darted into the passage, and, listening for one moment at the foot of the stairs, walked up.

At the second flight a door opened and a woman looked out, but Spazzola's face looked so calm and his step was so staid and unflurried that the woman's suspicions, if she had any, were allayed, and, muttering "Going up to the top, I suppose," withdrew her head and slammed the door.

As he neared the top landing, the Italian's footsteps became almost noiseless, and, bending forward, he stole up the stairs like a cat, his hand instinctively grasping the handle of the stiletto beneath his cloak.

Given a background of some rotten Italian palace instead of the faded paper of the dingy staircase and he would have made an interesting picture.

"This must be it," he muttered, as he stooped down at the keyhole of the door. "Almost dark. Can see no one. I will knock. Courage, Spazzola; this may lead to business," and he knocked softly at the door.

No answer.

He waited for two minutes and knocked again, this time louder.

Still no answer.

Then he listened breathlessly, and, hearing nothing, tried the handle of the door.

It was locked.

"Soh!" he muttered, "my sweet child was wrong for once. This owl does fly by day. I am curious. It is a mere plaything, this lock. Pah! We will for amusement—mark me, only amusement—take one peep at the owl's nest."

With a smile that lit up his face like a flash of sunlight, and showed his glittering teeth, he took from his pocket a small steel instrument, inserted it in the keyhole, turned it with a peculiar twist of the hand, and opened the door.

An exclamation of astonishment burst from his lips as the interior of the room met his view. Beside the plain table and chair, piece of square carpet, and poverty-stricken aspect, the room, though utterly devoid of anything approaching comfort in the way of furniture, was furnished in one corner with an easel, upon which shone the commencement of what promised to be a superb study of an old country house. On the walls glistened a number of unframed pictures, women's heads, bits of landscape, a scene from one of Racine's plays, a scrap of forest foliage, and the portrait of a superb mastiff, all bearing about them the evidence of a master-hand, which the Italian, no mean critic, detected at a glance.

On the plain deal table, lying beside palettes and brushes, was a cup of water and a crust of bread.

Taking off his hat with an air of profound respect, Spazzola entered.

"It is superb," he murmured, "superb. I have found a Carlo Dolci, a Titian, a Rubens, a—St. Peter! what colours! what forms! It is magnificent. Spazzolo, thou art in a great man's studio. Tread softly. Dry bread and water! Oh, genius, thou dost always starve, and thus, being light, canst float to heaven, while heavier souls are chained to earth. And this," he continued, going to the easel, "this is —ah, Marie! what is this? These leaves! this sky! It is he! At last! My soul, keep thou within my bosom. I have him at last! Spazzola," he cried, throwing up his hands in a frenzy of delight, "thou art not mistaken. Thy prey is in thy grasp. St. Marie! If Felise could see this and these," waving his arms towards the pictures, "would she not die of joy, of malice, of desire? At last! at last! Oh, monsieur, milord, duke, or whatever they call you, Spazzola's claws are round thy throat and purse!"

END OF VOL I.